Table of Conte

Map Legends

Since space was at a premium in this book, we elected not to put a map legend on every page. Shown below are all the symbols you will need throughout the book. You will need to refer to it as you complete each page. Some of the symbols are used over and over. Those that are used solely for one specific state are labeled with the postal abbreviations of the state.

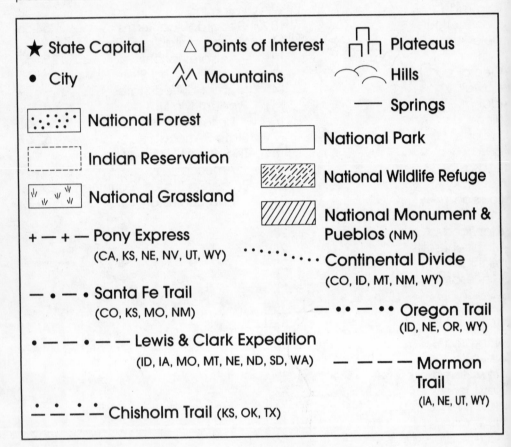

★ State Capital   △ Points of Interest   Plateaus

• City   Mountains   Hills

———— Springs

National Forest

National Park

Indian Reservation

National Wildlife Refuge

National Grassland

National Monument & Pueblos (NM)

+ — + — Pony Express
(CA, KS, NE, NV, UT, WY)

Continental Divide
(CO, ID, MT, NM, WY)

— • — • Santa Fe Trail
(CO, KS, MO, NM)

Oregon Trail
(ID, NE, OR, WY)

• — — • — — Lewis & Clark Expedition
(ID, IA, MO, MT, NE, ND, SD, WA)

Mormon Trail
(IA, NE, UT, WY)

Chisholm Trail (KS, OK, TX)

United States Map

The map (on page 3) of the United States with the state boundaries and the state capitals will be a handy resource for you as you work through the book. It will help you understand the location of each state in relation to the country as a whole.

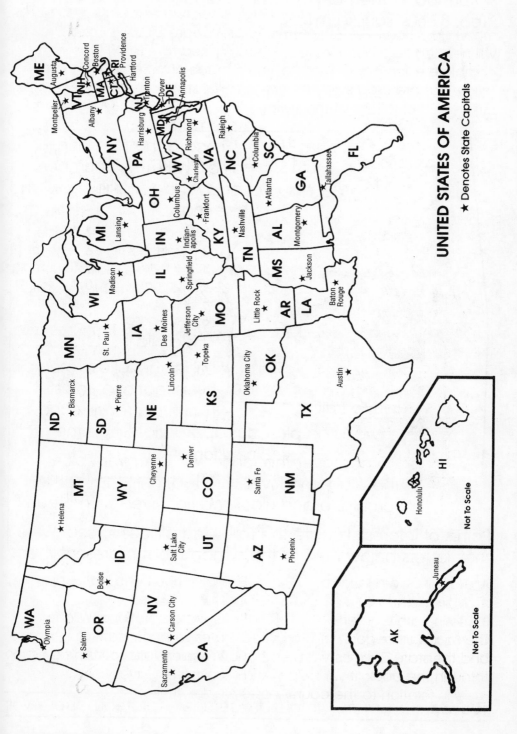

UNITED STATES OF AMERICA
★ Denotes State Capitals

Alabama

Postal Abbreviation: AL

Statehood: December 14, 1819 – 22nd
Area: 51,609 square miles

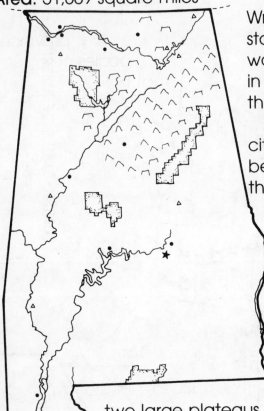

Write the names of the states, rivers and body of water that border Alabama in their correct locations on the map.

Locate the following cities. Write their numbers below next to their dots on the map.

1. Mobile
2. Birmingham
3. Huntsville
4. Montgomery
5. Selma
6. Tuscaloosa
7. Sheffield
8. Florence
9. Tuscumbia
10. Tuskegee
11. Decatur

The capital is _____.

Label the lakes, reservoir, rivers, national forests, mountain ranges and two large plateaus appropriately on the map.

Trace over the Tennessee River with blue, the Alabama River with red, and the Mobile, Tombigee and Black Warrior Rivers with green.

Points of Interest: Locate the following places to see. Write their letters below next to the symbols that represent them.

A. Russell Cave National Monument
B. Bellingrath Gardens
C. Mound State Park
D. Cathedral Caverns
E. Horseshoe Bend National Military Park
F. Choctaw National Wildlife Refuge
G. Wheeler National Wildlife Refuge
H. Saltpeter Caves

Words: cavern   mound   refuge   plateau   reservoir

Alaska

Postal Abbreviation: AK

Statehood: January 3, 1959 – 49th
Area: 599,757 square miles

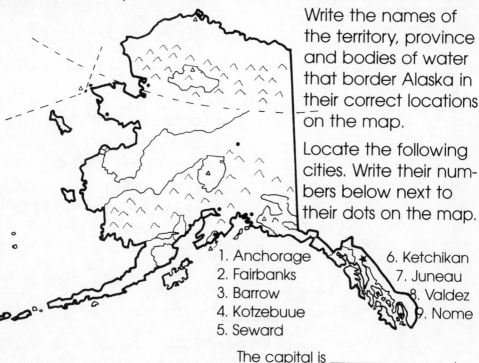

Write the names of the territory, province and bodies of water that border Alaska in their correct locations on the map.

Locate the following cities. Write their numbers below next to their dots on the map.

1. Anchorage
2. Fairbanks
3. Barrow
4. Kotzebuue
5. Seward
6. Ketchikan
7. Juneau
8. Valdez
9. Nome

The capital is _____.

Label the mountain ranges, river, national parks and Alexander Archipelago appropriately on the map. Circle the Aleutian Islands. Mark an **X** on Kodiak Island. Trace over the International Dateline with red. Trace over the Arctic Circle with green. Mark an **S** on Seward Peninsula.

Points of Interest: Locate the following places to see. Write their letters below next to the symbols that represent them.

A. Mount McKinley
B. Anaktuvuk Pass
C. Diomede Islands
D. Point Barrow Naval Arctic Research Laboratory
E. Trans Alaska Pipeline
F. Sitka National Historic Park
G. Kenai Fiords National Park

Words: glacier   arctic   aleut   archipelago   fjord

Arizona

Postal Abbreviation: AZ

Statehood: February 14, 1912 – 48th
Area: 113,909 square miles

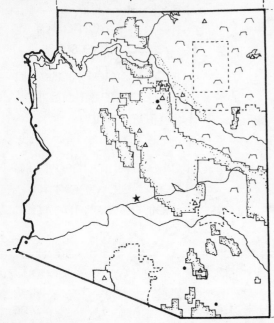

Write the names of the states, river and country that border Arizona in their correct locations on the map.

Color the Grand Canyon grey.

Locate the following cities. Write their numbers below next to their dots on the map.

1. Tucson
2. Phoenix
3. Flagstaff
4. Yuma
5. Tombstone
6. Lake Havasu City

The capital is _____ .

Label the rivers, lake and national forests appropriately on the map. Mark an **X** on the Navajo Indian Reservation, a **Y** on the Papago Indian Reservation and a **Z** on the Fort Apache and San Carlos Indian Reservations. Circle the Hopi Indian Reservation.

Points of Interest: Locate the following places to see. Write their letters below next to the symbols that represent them.

A. Canyon de Chelly National Monument
B. Painted Desert
C. Petrified Forest National Park
D. Montezuma Castle National Monument
E. Tonto National Monument
F. Organ Pipe Cactus National Monument
G. Tuzigoot National Monument
H. Hoover Dam
I. Navajo National Monument
J. Saguaro National Monument
K. Walnut Canyon
L. Sunset Crater
M. Wupatki

Words: saguaro canyon desert cactus reservation

Arkansas

Postal Abbreviation: AR

Statehood: June 15, 1836 – 25th
Area: 53,104

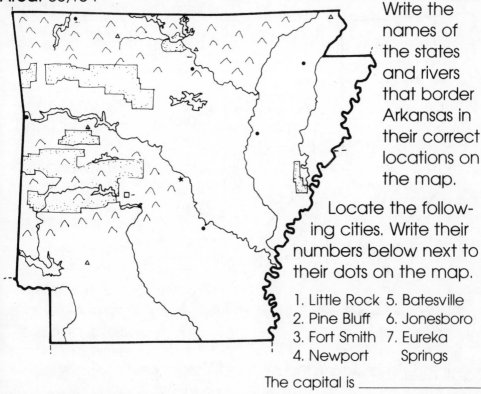

Write the names of the states and rivers that border Arkansas in their correct locations on the map.

Locate the following cities. Write their numbers below next to their dots on the map.

1. Little Rock
2. Pine Bluff
3. Fort Smith
4. Newport
5. Batesville
6. Jonesboro
7. Eureka Springs

The capital is _____.

Label the rivers, lakes, mountain ranges and national forests appropriately on the map.

Circle Hot Springs National Park, mark a line through Eureka Springs and mark an **X** on Blanchard Springs Caverns.

Points of Interest: Locate the following places to see. Write their letters below next to the symbols that represent them.

A. Magazine Mountain
B. Dog Patch U.S.A.
C. Crater of Diamonds
D. Chalk Bluff
E. Calico Rock

Words: springs bluff crater

California

Postal Abbreviation: CA

Statehood: September 9, 1850 – 31st

Area: 158,693 square miles

Write the names of the states, bodies of water and country that border California in their correct locations on the map.

Locate the following cities. Write their numbers below next to their dots on the map.

1. Los Angeles
2. Long Beach
3. San Diego
4. San Bernardino
5. Fresno

6. San Francisco
7. San Jose
8. Oakland
9. Sacramento

The capital is _____.

Label the rivers, mountain ranges, valleys, national parks and national monuments on the map.

Trace over the Pony Express with orange. Write a **T** on Lake Tahoe, an **M** on Mono Lake and an **S** on Shasta Lake. Circle the Salton Sea. Mark an **X** on the Mohave Desert. Color the valleys green.

Points of Interest: Locate the following places to see. Write their letters below next to the symbols that represent them.

A. Golden Gate National Recreation Area
B. Pinnacles National Monument
C. Mount Shasta
D. Mount Whitney
E. Muir Woods National Monument

F. Devil's Post Pile National Monument
G. Monterery Peninsula
H. Edwards Air Force Base
I. Point Arena
J. Lava Beds National Monument

Words: channel   sequoia   lava   point   valley

Colorado

Postal Abbreviation: CO

Statehood: August 1, 1876 – 38th
Area: 104,247 square miles

Write the names of the states that border Colorado in their correct locations on the map.

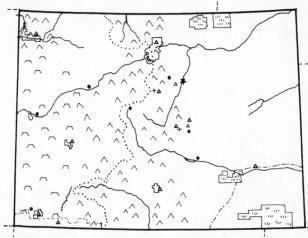

Locate the following cities. Write their numbers below next to their dots on the map.

1. Grand Junction
2. Denver
3. Cortez
4. Pueblo
5. Colorado Springs
6. Boulder
7. Glenwood Springs
8. Leadville

The capital is _____ .

Label the mountain range, grasslands, rivers, creeks, reservoir, and lakes on the map.

Trace the Santa Fe Trail with red, the Continental Divide with green, the Royal Gorge with brown and the Narrow Gauge Railroad with blue. Make an **X** to locate Curango and a **Y** for Silverton.

Points of Interest: Locate the following places. Write their letters below next to the symbols that represent them.

A. Mesa Verde National Park
B. Great Sand Dunes National Monument
C. Black Canyon of the Gunnison National Monument
D. Dinosaur National Monument
E. Rocky Mountain National Park
F. Ute Indian Reservation
G. U.S. Air Force Academy
H. Pike's Peak
I. Garden of the Gods
J. Bent's Fort
K. Central City
L. Mt. Evans

Words: peak   canyon   fork   mesa   pass

Connecticut

Postal Abbreviation: CT

Statehood: January 9, 1788 – 5th

Area: 5,009 square miles

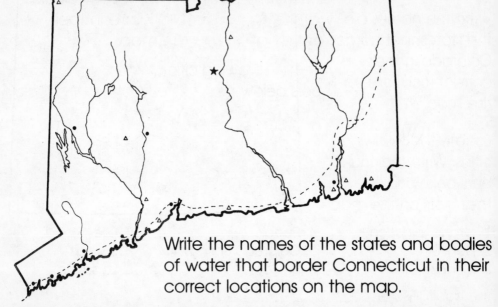

Write the names of the states and bodies of water that border Connecticut in their correct locations on the map.

Locate the following cities. Write their numbers below next to their dots on the map.

1. Stamford
2. Bridgeport
3. Hartford
4. New Haven
5. Waterbury
6. Greenwich
7. New London
8. New Milford
9. Norwalk

The capital is _____ .

Label the rivers and lakes on the map. Trace over the Connecticut Turnpike with blue. Circle New Haven Harbor. Mark an **X** on the Norwalk Islands.

Points of Interest: Locate the following places. Write their letters below next to the symbols that represent them.

A. Old Town Mill
B. Fort Griswold and Groton Monument
C. Mystic Seaport
D. Mount Frissell
E. Whitfield House
F. Trolley Museums
G. Glebe House
H. Mansfield House

Words: hollow   harbor   sound   knoll

Delaware

Postal Abbreviation: DE

Statehood: December 7 – 1st
Area: 2,057 square miles

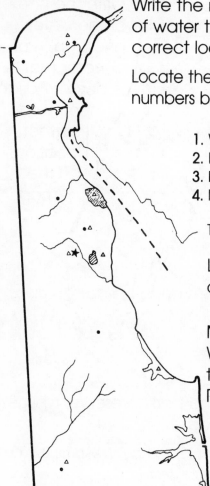

Write the names of the states and bodies of water that border Delaware in their correct locations on the map.

Locate the following cities. Write their numbers below next to their dots on the map.

1. Wilmington
2. Newark
3. Dover
4. Milford

5. Laurel
6. Cowgill Corner
7. Delaware City
8. Smyrna

The capital is _____

Label the rivers, bays and canal on the map.

Mark an **X** on Cape Henlopen. Write the name of the state on the east side of the Delaware River where it is located.

Points of Interest: Locate the following places. Write their letters below next to the symbols that represent them.

A. Winterthur Museum
B. Prime Hook National Wildlife Refuge
C. Bombay Hook National Wildlife Refuge
D. Dover Air Force Base

E. Old Swede Church
F. Old State House
G. Fort Delaware
H. Great Cypress Swamp
I. Octagonal Schoolhouse

Words: bay   cape   swamp   canal   cypress   hook

Florida

Statehood: March 3, 1845 – 27th
Area: 58,560 square miles

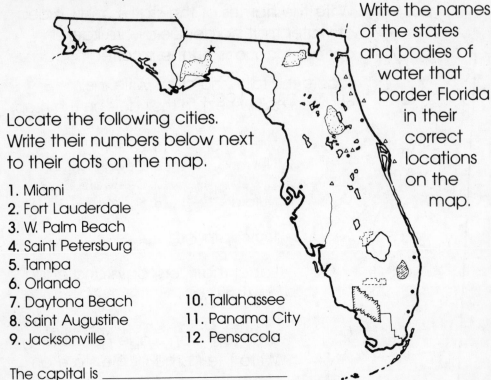

Write the names of the states and bodies of water that border Florida in their correct locations on the map.

Locate the following cities. Write their numbers below next to their dots on the map.

1. Miami
2. Fort Lauderdale
3. W. Palm Beach
4. Saint Petersburg
5. Tampa
6. Orlando
7. Daytona Beach
8. Saint Augustine
9. Jacksonville
10. Tallahassee
11. Panama City
12. Pensacola

The capital is _____

Label the rivers, national forests and park, preserve, refuge and Indian reservations on the map.

Circle Lake Okeechobee. Mark an **X** on Key West. Draw a line from Charlotte Harbor to Tampa Bay.

Points of Interest: Locate the following places. Write their letters below next to the symbols that represent them.

A. John F. Kennedy Space Center
B. Cape Canaveral
C. Cypress Gardens
D. Marineland
E. Fort Matanzas National Monument
F. Castillo de San Marcos National Monument
G. Seaworld and Disney World

Words: key   strait   gulf   harbor

Georgia

Postal Abbreviation: GA

Statehood: January 2, 1788 – 4th
Area: 58,876 square miles

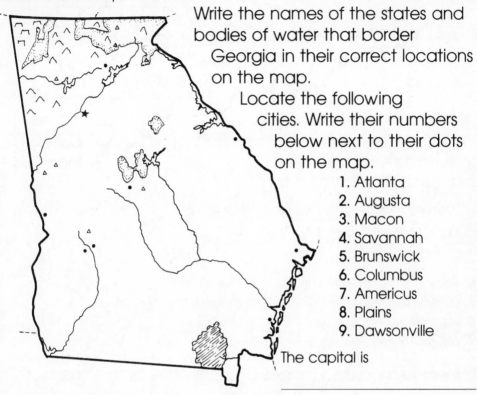

Write the names of the states and bodies of water that border Georgia in their correct locations on the map.

Locate the following cities. Write their numbers below next to their dots on the map.

1. Atlanta
2. Augusta
3. Macon
4. Savannah
5. Brunswick
6. Columbus
7. Americus
8. Plains
9. Dawsonville

The capital is

_____.

Label the rivers, lakes, reservoirs, national forests and refuge on the map.

Color the Appalachian Mountains blue and the Piedmont Plateau green.

Points of Interest: Locate the following places. Write their letters below next to the symbols that represent them.

A. Andersonville National Historic Site
B. Callaway Gardens
C. Little White House
D. Etowah Mounds
E. Dahlonega Gold Museum
F. Toccoa Falls
G. Brasstown Bald Mountain
H. Ocmulgee National Monument

Words: falls   mound

Hawaii

Postal Abbreviation: HI

Statehood: August 21, 1959 – 50th
Area: 6,450 square miles

Name the islands
that comprise Hawaii
and the body of water
that surrounds them.

Locate the following cities. Write their
numbers below next to their dots on
the map.

1. Hilo   3. Koele   5. Honolulu
2. Wailuku   4. Maunaloa   6. Wailua

The capital is _____ .

Label the mountain ranges and channels on the map.

Color Hawaii Volcanoes National Park green and Haleakala
National Park orange.

Points of Interest: Locate the following places. Write their
letters below next to the symbols that represent them.

A. Kalapana Black Sand Beach
B. Kealakekua Bay
C. Pearl Harbor
D. Waimea Canyon
E. Royal Mausoleum
F. Mauna Loa Volcano
G. Kilauea Crater
H. Mauna Kea

Words: crater   island   volcano   beach   atoll

Idaho

Postal Abbreviation: ID

Statehood: July 3, 1890 – 43rd
Area: 83,557 square miles

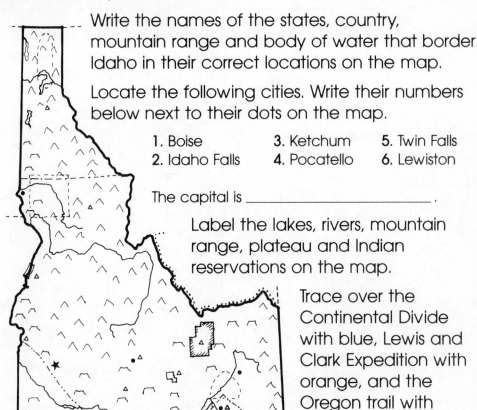

Write the names of the states, country, mountain range and body of water that border Idaho in their correct locations on the map.

Locate the following cities. Write their numbers below next to their dots on the map.

1. Boise
2. Idaho Falls
3. Ketchum
4. Pocatello
5. Twin Falls
6. Lewiston

The capital is _____.

Label the lakes, rivers, mountain range, plateau and Indian reservations on the map.

Trace over the Continental Divide with blue, Lewis and Clark Expedition with orange, and the Oregon trail with brown.

Points of Interest: Locate the following places. Write their letters below next to the symbols that represent them.

A. Cataldo Mission
B. Hells Canyon
C. Fort Boise
D. National Reactor Testing Station
E. Craters of the Moon National Monument
F. Sun Valley
G. Cities of Rock (2)
H. Pilot Knob
I. Shoshone Falls
J. Balanced Rock
K. Old Fort Hall

Words: salmon   sawtooth   knob

Illinois

Postal Abbreviation: IL

Statehood: December 3, 1818 – 21st
Area: 56,400 square miles

Write the names of the states and bodies of water that border Illinois in their correct locations on the map.

Locate the following cities. Write their numbers below next to their dots on the map.

1. Chicago
2. Rock Island
3. Moline
4. Rockford
5. Oregon
6. Peoria
7. Pekin
8. Nauvoo
9. Quincy
10. Springfield
11. Champaign-Urbana
12. E. St. Louis

The capital is _____.

Label all the bodies of water and the national forest.
Circle Kaskaskia Island. Mark an **X** at the confluence of the Mississippi and Ohio Rivers.

Color the Central Plains area green and the Shawnee Hills orange. Make an **X** where St. Louis is located.

Points of Interest: Locate the following places. Write their letters next to the symbols that represent them.

A. Bishop Hill
B. Black Hawk Statue
C. Lincoln's New Salem State Park
D. Dickson Mounds State Memorial
E. Vandalia State House
F. Ulysses Grant Home
G. Cahokia Mound State Park

Words: plain   confluence

Indiana

Postal Abbreviation: IN

Statehood: December 11, 1816 – 19th
Area: 36,291 square miles

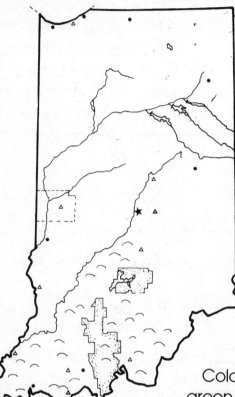

Write the names of the states and bodies of water that border Indiana in their correct locations on the map.

Locate the following cities. Write their numbers below next to their dots on the map.

1. Gary
2. Michigan City
3. South Bend
4. Fort Wayne
5. Muncie
6. Indianapolis
7. Terre Haute
8. Evansville
9. Santa Claus

The capital is _____ .

Label all the bodies of water on the map.

Color Hoosier National Forest green and Parke County pink. Put a triangle where Louisville is located. Trace over the Indiana Toll Road with orange.

Points of Interest: Locate the following places. Write their letters below next to the symbols that represent them.

A. Lincoln Boyhood National Memorial
B. Wyandotte Cave
C. William Henry Harrison Home
D. One of thirty covered bridges in country
E. Indiana Dunes National Lakeshore
F. Brown County Art Galleries
G. Conner Prairie Pioneer Settlement
H. James Whitcomb Riley Home
I. Lincoln Pioneer Village
J. New Harmony Historic District

Words: Hoosier   creek

Iowa

Statehood: December 28, 1846 – 29th
Area: 56,290 square miles

Write the names of the states and rivers that border Iowa in their correct locations on the map.

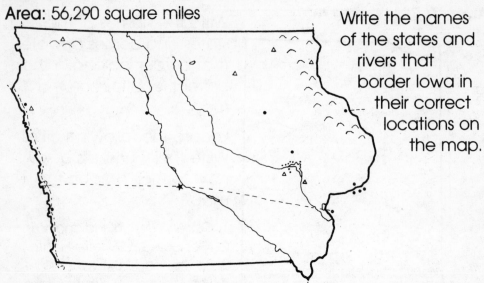

Locate the following cities. Write their numbers below next to their dots on the map.

1. Des Moines
2. Davenport
3. Nauvoo (IL)
4. Dubuque

5. Fort Dodge
6. Sioux City
7. Council Bluffs
8. Cedar Rapids

9. Waterloo
The capital is

_____ .

Label the rivers, lake, and the three cities across the river from Davenport.

Mark an **X** at the confluence of the Big Sioux and the Missouri Rivers, and a **Y** at the confluence of the Mississippi and Des Moines Rivers. Trace over the Lewis and Clark Expedition with orange and the Mormon Trail with black.

Points of Interest: Locate the following places. Write their letters below next to the symbols that represent them.

A. Effigy Mounds
   National Monument
B. Ocheyedan Mound
C. Amana Colonies

D. Herbert Hoover National
   Historic Site
E. Little Brown Church
F. Dvorak Memorial
G. Floyd Monument

Words: effigy   expedition

Kansas

Postal Abbreviation: KS

Statehood: January 29, 1861 – 34th
Area: 82,264 square miles

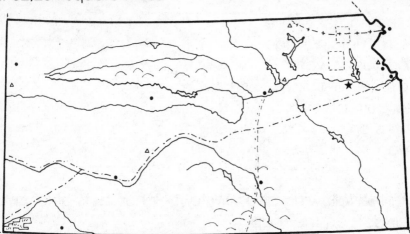

Write the names of the states and body of water that border Kansas in their correct location on the map.

Locate the following cities. Write their numbers below next to their dots on the map.

1. Dodge City
2. Wichita
3. Topeka

4. Leavenworth
5. Abilene
6. Hays

7. Goodland
8. Liberal
9. Kansas City, KS

The capital is _____ .

Label the bodies of water, Smoky Hills, Flint Hills and grassland area on the map.

Mark an **X** on St. Joseph, Missouri. Color the Indian reservations green. Trace the Santa Fe Trail red, the Pony Express brown and the Chisholm Trail grey.

Points of Interest: Locate the following places. Write their letters below next to the symbols that represent them.

A. Mount Sunflower
B. Fort Leavenworth
C. Fort Larned National
   Historic Site

D. Eisenhower Library and
   Museum
E. Fort Riley
F. Hollenberg Station

Words: flint   hill   tornado

Kentucky

Postal Abbreviation: KY

Statehood: June 1, 1792 – 15th
Area: 40,395 square miles

Write the names of the states, mountain range and bodies of water that border Kentucky in their correct locations on the map.

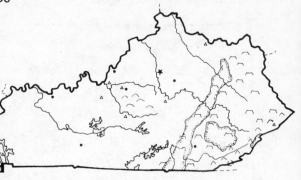

Locate the following cities. Write their numbers below next to their dots on the map.

1. Lexington
2. Frankfort
3. Louisville
4. Paducah
5. Owensboro
6. Bowling Green
7. Bardstown
8. Corbin

The capital is _____ .

Label the bodies of water, the Knobs and the national forest on the map.

Color the Cumberland Plateau green, the Pine Mountains blue and the Cumberland Mountains orange. Mark an **X** on the Cumberland Gap National Historic Park.

Points of Interest: Locate the following places. Write their letters below next to the symbols that represent them.

A. Breaks of the Sandy
B. Barkley Dam
C. Mammoth Cave National Park
D. Fort Knox
E. Land Between the Lakes
F. My Old Kentucky Home
G. Abraham Lincoln Birthplace National Historic Site
H. Washington
I. Constitution Square
J. Elizabethtown

Words: dam   hollow   gap

Louisiana

Postal Abbreviation: LA

Statehood: April 30, 1812 – 18th
Area: 48,523 square miles

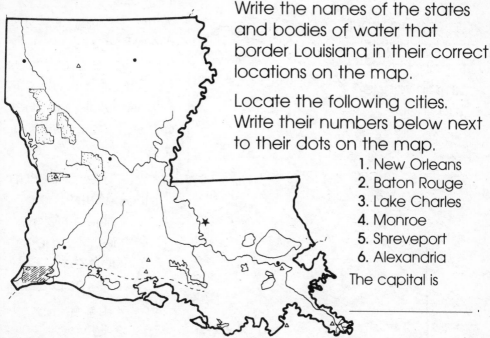

Write the names of the states and bodies of water that border Louisiana in their correct locations on the map.

Locate the following cities. Write their numbers below next to their dots on the map.

1. New Orleans
2. Baton Rouge
3. Lake Charles
4. Monroe
5. Shreveport
6. Alexandria

The capital is

_____

Label the lakes, reservoir, national forest and rivers on the map.

Trace over the Intercoastal Waterway with red. Color the Sabine National Wildlife Refuge green. Draw a line from Lake Borgne to Barataria Bay to Vermillion Bay.

Points of Interest: Locate the following places. Write their letters below next to the symbols that represent them.

A. Evangeline Oak
B. Avery Island
C. Driskill Mountain
D. Mississippi Delta
E. Jean Lafitte National Historic Park and Reserve
F. Grand Isle
G. Fort Polk Military Reservation

Words: bayou   delta

Maine

Postal Abbreviation: ME

Statehood: March 15, 1820 – 23rd
Area: 33,215 square miles

Label the national forest, bodies of water and main mountain range on the map.

Write the names of the state, bodies of water and provinces of Canada that border Maine in their correct locations on the map.

Locate the following cities. Write their numbers below next to their dots on the map.

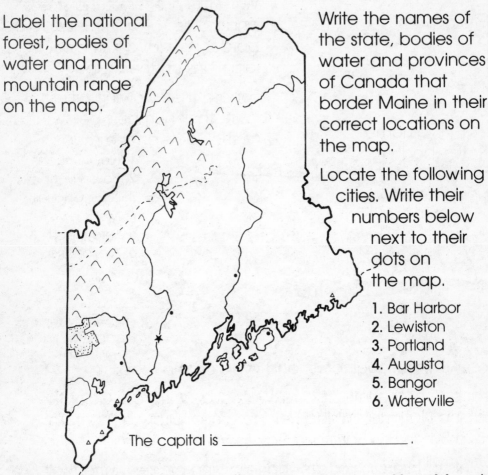

1. Bar Harbor
2. Lewiston
3. Portland
4. Augusta
5. Bangor
6. Waterville

The capital is _____.

Trace the Appalachian Trail with yellow. Mark an **X** on Mount Desert Island. Draw a line from Frenchman Bay to Penobscot Bay to Casco Bay. Color the Aroostook Plain green.

Points of Interest: Locate the following places. Write their letters below next to the symbols that represent them.

A. Old Goal Museum
B. Burnham Tavern
C. Wedding Cake House
D. Acadia National Park
E. Tate House

Words: coastal   province plain

Maryland

Postal Abbreviation: MD

Statehood: April 28 , 1788 – 7th
Area: 10,577 square miles

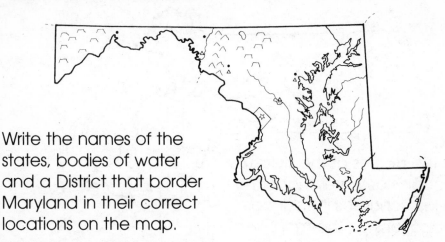

Write the names of the states, bodies of water and a District that border Maryland in their correct locations on the map.

Locate the following cities. Write their numbers below next to their dots on the map.

1. Baltimore
2. Washington, D.C.
3. Annapolis
4. Cumberland
5. Hagerstown
6. Frederick

The capital is _____ .

Label the two mountain ranges, two plateaus and the rivers on the map.

Color all of Chesapeake Bay blue. Color the District of Columbia red. Mark an X on the nation's capital.

Points of Interest: Locate the following places. Write their letters below next to the symbols that represent them.

A. Kent Island
B. Assateague Island National Sea Shore
C. Antietam National Battlefield Site
D. Barbara Fritchie House
E. U.S. Naval Academy
F. Fort McHenry
G. Patuxent Wildlife Refuge

Words: branch   district

Massachusetts

Postal Abbreviation: MA

Statehood: February 6, 1788 – 6th
Area: 8,257 square miles

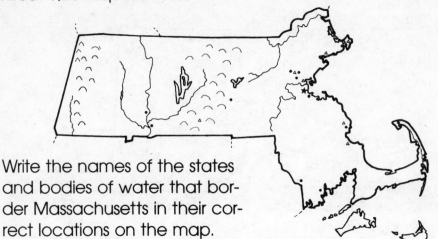

Write the names of the states and bodies of water that border Massachusetts in their correct locations on the map.

Label the reservoirs, rivers, Nantucket and Martha's Vineyard.

Locate the following cities. Write their numbers below next to their dots on the map.

1. Fall River
2. Duxbury
3. Provincetown
4. Quincy
5. New Bedford
6. Boston
7. Cambridge
8. Lexington
9. Concord
10. Worcester
11. Springfield
12. Holyoke

The capital is _____ .

Color the Berkshire Hills green, the Taconic Mountains orange, the Western Uplands or Berkshire Valley grey, the Connecticut Valley or Lowland pink, the Eastern Uplands brown and the Coastal Uplands yellow.

Points of Interest: Locate the following places. Write their letters below next to the symbols that represent them.

A. Harvard University
B. Minute Man National Historic Park
C. John Alden House
D. Mayflower II
E. Fisherman's Memorial
F. Old Sturbridge Village
G. Witch's House

Words: upland   lowland

Michigan

Postal Abbreviation: MI

Statehood: January 26, 1837 – 26th
Area: 58,216 square miles

Locate the following cities. Write their numbers below next to their dots on the map.

1. Lansing
2. Ann Arbor
3. Detroit
4. Flint
5. Grand Rapids
6. Kalamazoo
7. Muskegon
8. Saginaw
9. Port Huron
10. Petoskey
11. Holland
12. Jackson

Write the names of the states, bodies of water and province of Canada that border Michigan in their correct locations on the map.

The capital is

_____

Label the national forests, bodies of water and mountain ranges.

Color the upper peninsula red. Circle Mackinac Island. Mark an **X** on Beaver Island. Draw a line through the Soo Canal and Locks.

Points of Interest: Locate the following places. Write their letters below next to the symbols that represent them.

A. Big Spring
B. Fort Michilimackinac
C. Greenfield Village
D. Isle Royale National Park
E. Sleeping Bear Dunes National Lakeshore

F. U.S. Ski Hall of Fame
G. Pictured Rocks National Lakeshore
H. L'Anse Indian Reservation

Words: canal   locks   peninsula

Minnesota

Postal Abbreviation: MN

Statehood: May 11, 1858 – 32nd
Area: 84,068 square miles

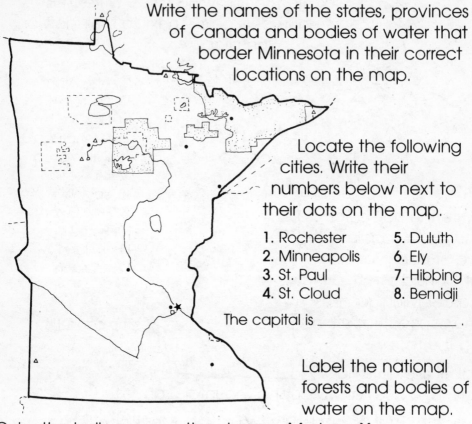

Write the names of the states, provinces of Canada and bodies of water that border Minnesota in their correct locations on the map.

Locate the following cities. Write their numbers below next to their dots on the map.

1. Rochester   **5.** Duluth
2. Minneapolis   **6.** Ely
3. St. Paul   **7.** Hibbing
4. St. Cloud   **8.** Bemidji

The capital is _____ .

Label the national forests and bodies of water on the map.

Color the Indian reservations brown. Mark an **X** on Voyageurs National Park.

Points of Interest: Locate the following places. Write their letters below next to the symbols that represent them.

A. The source of the Mississippi River
B. Pipestone National Monument
C. Grand Portage National Monument
D. Paul Bunyan and Babe statues
E. Northernmost Point of U.S. other than Alaska
F. International Falls

Words: international   portage   source

Mississippi

Postal Abbreviation: MS

Statehood: December 10, 1817 – 20th
Area: 47,716 square miles

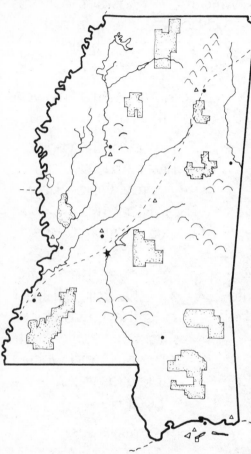

Write the names of the states and bodies of water that border Mississippi in their correct locations on the map.

Locate the following cities. Write their numbers below next to their dots on the map.

1. Natchez	6. Greenwood
2. Fayette	7. Tupelo
3. Jackson	8. Columbus
4. Flora	9. Hattiesburg
5. Vicksburg	10. Biloxi

The capital is

_____.

Label the bodies of water and national forests on the map.

Color the Pine Hill Region green, the Red Hill Region red, the Black Belt Region black, the Bluff Hill Region tan and the Pontoto Ridge orange. Trace the Nachez Trace Parkway with a pencil. Circle the Yazoo Basin.

Points of Interest: Locate the following places. Write their letters below next to the symbols that represent them.

A. Vicksburg
B. Elvis Presley Birthplace
C. Petrified Forest
D. Choctaw Indian Reservation

E. Florewood River Planation
F. Mount Locust
G. Ship Island
H. Old Spanish Fort

Words: basin   ridge   belt

Missouri

Postal Abbreviation: MO

Statehood: August 10, 1821 – 24th
Area: 69,686 square miles

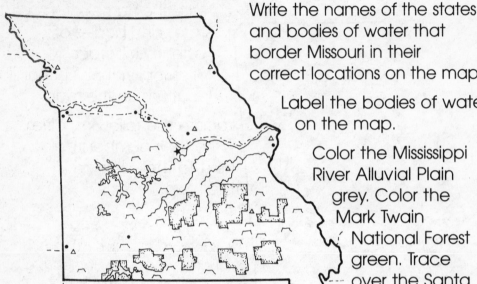

Write the names of the states and bodies of water that border Missouri in their correct locations on the map.

Label the bodies of water on the map.

Color the Mississippi River Alluvial Plain grey. Color the Mark Twain National Forest green. Trace over the Santa Fe Trail with red and the Lewis and Clark Expedition with brown. Circle what is nicknamed the "Boot Heel".

The capital is

_____.

Locate the following cities. Write their numbers below next to their dots on the map.

1. St. Joseph
2. St. Louis
3. Kansas City
4. Jefferson City
5. Springfield
6. Independence
7. Joplin
8. Columbia
9. Franklin
10. Hannibal
11. Fulton
12. Arrow Rock

Points of Interest: Locate the following places. Write their letters below next to the symbols that represent them.

A. George Washington Carver National Monument
B. Winston Churchill Memorial and Library
C. Pony Express Stables
D. Mark Twain Home and Museum
E. Meramec Caverns
F. Jefferson National Expansion Memorial - The Gateway Arch
G. Anderson House
H. Truman Library
I. Elephant Rocks

Words: alluvial   mill

Montana

Postal Abbreviation: MT

Statehood: November 8, 1889 – 41st
Area: 147,138 square miles

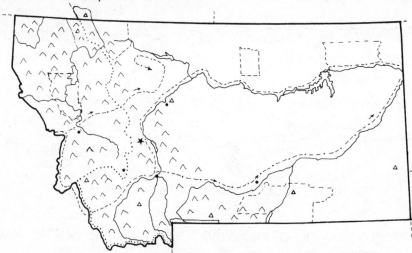

Write the names of the states and the provinces of Canada that border Montana in their correct locations on the map.

Locate the following cities. Write their numbers below next to their dots on the map.

1. Missoula
2. Helena
3. Great Falls

4. Butte
5. Three Forks
6. Billings

The capital is

_____ .

Label the bodies of water, mountain range and Indian reservation on the map.

Trace over the Lewis and Clark Expedition with brown and the Continental Divide with blue.

Points of Interest: Locate the following places. Write their letters below next to the symbols that represent them.

A. Virginia City
B. Giant Springs
C. Granite Peak
D. Big Hole Battlefield National Monument
E. Glacier National Park

F. Waterton Glacier International Peace Park
G. Custer Battlefield National Monument
H. Medicine Rocks

Words: butte   granite

Nebraska

Statehood: March 1, 1867 – 37th
Area: 77,227 square miles

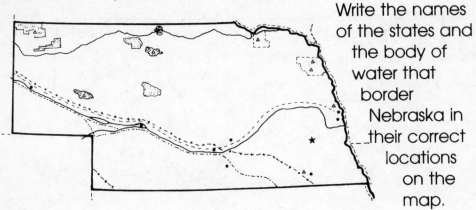

Write the names of the states and the body of water that border Nebraska in their correct locations on the map.

Locate the following cities. Write their numbers below next to their dots on the map.

1. Scottbluff
2. Hastings
3. Lincoln
4. Omaha
5. Bellevue
6. Kearney
7. Grand Island
8. North Platte
9. Beatrice

The capital is _____ .

Label the bodies of water, national forests and national grasslands on the map.

Trace over the Oregon Trail with green, the Morman Trail with purple, the Pony Express with orange and the Lewis and Clark Expedition with brown.

Points of Interest: Locate the following places. Write their letters below next to the symbols that represent them.

A. Homestead National Monument of America
B. Omaha Indian Reservation
C. Winnebago Indian Reservation
D. Santee Indian Reservation
E. Toadstool Park
F. Valentine National Wildlife Refuge
G. Fort Niobrara National Wildlife Refuge
H. Crescent Lake National Wildlife Refuge
I. Boys Town

Words: agate   fossil

30

Nevada

Postal Abbreviation: NV

Statehood: October 31, 1864 – 36th
Area: 110,540 square miles

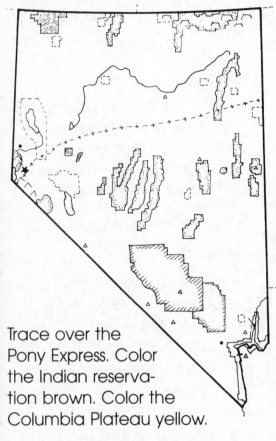

Write the names of the states and bodies of water that border Nevada in their correct locations on the map.

Locate the following cities. Write their numbers below next to their dots on the map.

1. Las Vegas
2. Reno
3. Carson City

The capital is

_____.

Trace over the Pony Express. Color the Indian reservation brown. Color the Columbia Plateau yellow.

Label the national forests and wildlife refuges, the Desert National Wildlife Range, the Sierra Nevada Mountain Range and the bodies of water on the map.

Points of Interest: Locate the following places. Write their letters below next to the symbols that represent them on the map.

A. Hoover Dam
B. Atomic Energy Commission Test Site
C. Valley of Fire State Park
D. Devils Hole

E. Boundary Peak
F. Lehman Caves National Monument
G. Ghost Towns: Rhyolite and Hamilton
H. Geyser Basin

Words: atomic   geyser   basin   range

31

New Hampshire

Postal Abbreviation: NH

Statehood: June 21, 1788 – 9th
Area: 9,304 square miles

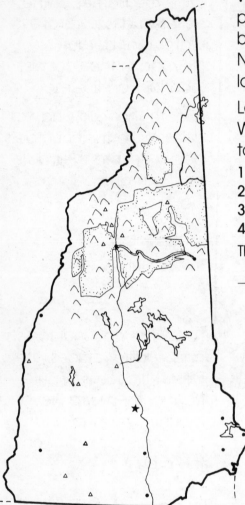

Write the names of the states, province of Canada and bodies of water that border New Hampshire in their correct locations on the map.

Locate the following cities. Write their numbers below next to their dots on the map.

1. Manchester
2. Concord
3. Nashua
4. Exeter

5. Portsmouth
6. Durham
7. Hanover
8. Keene

The capital is

_____ .

Label the bodies of water, national forest and mountain range on the map.

Color the Eastern New England Uplands grey, the Coastal Lowlands yellow and the mountain green. Draw the Kancamagus Highway between Lincoln and Conway with red.

Points of Interest: Locate the following places. Write their letters below next to the symbols that represent them.

A. Mount Washington Cog Railway
B. Flume
C. Lost River
D. Franconia Notch

E. Saint-Gaudens National Historic Site
F. Wapack National Wildlife Refuge the Pines

Words: stream   monadnock   chasm   notch

New Jersey

Postal Abbreviation: NJ

Statehood: December 18, 1787 – 3rd
Area: 7,836 square miles

Write the names of the states and bodies of water that border New Jersey in their correct locations on the map.

Locate the following cities. Write their numbers below next to their dots on the map.

1. Atlantic City
2. Camden
3. Trenton
4. New Jersey
5. Newark
6. Elizabeth
7. New Brunswick
8. Morristown
9. Hackettstown
10. Paterson
11. Vineland
12. Millville

The capital is

_____.

Label the bodies of water and the Delaware Water Gap National Recreation Area on the map.

Color the Appalachian Ridge and Valley green, the New England Uplands orange, the Piedmont Plateau brown and the Atlantic Coastal Plain grey.

Points of Interest: Locate the following places. Write their letters below next to the symbols that represent them.

A. Barnegat Lighthouse
B. Great Egg Harbor Inlet
C. Delaware Water Gap
D. Sandy Hook
E. Fort Dix
F. Birthplace of naval officer, James Lawrence, ``Don't give up the ship.''
G. High Point
H. Walt Whitman House

Words: hook   harbor   inlet

New Mexico

Postal Abbreviation: NM

Statehood: January 6, 1912 – 47th
Area: 121,666 square miles

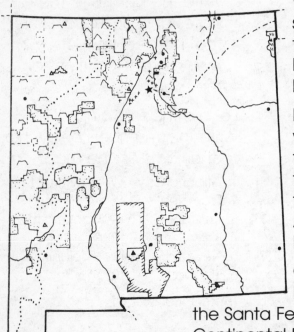

Write the names of the states and country that border New Mexico in their correct locations on the map.

Label the bodies of water, the national forests and grassland, the military range and the Navajo, Zuni, and Apache Indian Reservations.

Circle the Indian Pueblos. Trace over the Santa Fe Trail with red and the Continental Divide with blue.

Locate the following cities. Write their numbers below next to their dots on the map.

1. Albuquerque
2. Santa Fe
3. Arroyo Hondo
4. Alamogordo
5. Taos
6. Raton
7. Las Vegas
8. Gallup
9. Las Crucas
10. Silver City
11. Roswell
12. Hobbs
13. Tucumcari

The capital is

_____

Points of Interest: Locate the following places. Write their letters below next to the symbols that represent them.

A. Aztec Ruins National Monument
B. Chaco Canyon National Monument
C. Bandelier National Monument
D. Los Alamos Museum
E. White Sands National Monument
F. Gila Wilderness
G. Carlsbad Caverns National Monument

Words: arroyo   rio   pueblo   grassland

New York

Postal Abbreviation: NY

Statehood: July 26, 1788 – 11th
Area: 49,576 square miles

Write the names of the states, provinces of Canada and bodies of water that border New York in their correct locations on the map.

Locate the following cities. Write their numbers below next to their dots on the map.

1. Poughkeepsie
2. New York City
3. Schenectady
4. Albany
5. Niagara Falls
6. Buffalo
7. Rochester
8. Syracuse
9. Watertown
10. Ithaca
11. Hampton Bay
12. Troy

The capital is _____ .

Label the bodies of water on the map.

Color the plateau region orange, the highland regions green and the lowland regions grey. Mark an **X** on Long Island. Circle Staten Island. Color the East River blue.

Points of Interest: Locate the following places. Write their letters below next to the symbols that represent them.

A. West Point; U.S. Military Academy
B. Statue of Liberty National Monument
C. Home of Franklin Delano Roosevelt National Historic Site
D. Fort Ticonderoga
E. Howe Caverns

Words: canal   sound   island   urban

North Carolina   Postal Abbreviation: NC

Statehood: November 21, 1789 – 12th
Area: 52,586 square miles

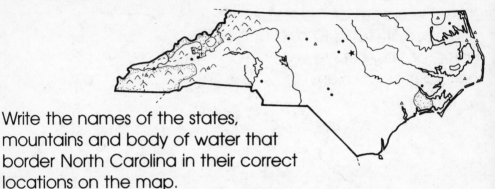

Write the names of the states, mountains and body of water that border North Carolina in their correct locations on the map.

Mark an **X** on Ocracoke Island. Circle Cape Fear.

Label the bodies of water, national forests and mountain ranges on the map.

Locate the following cities. Write their numbers below next to their dots on the map.

1. Asheville
2. Montreat
3. Charlotte
4. Winston-Salem
5. Greensboro
6. Raleigh
7. Durham
8. Chapel Hill
9. New Bern
10. Pinehurst
11. Fort Bragg
12. Elizabeth City

The capital is _____ .

Points of Interest: Locate the following places. Write their letters below next to the symbols that represent them.

A. Cape Lejeune Marine Corps Base
B. Great Dismal Swamp National Wildlife Refuge
C. Pamlico Sound
D. Albemarle Sound
E. Wright Brothers National Monument
F. Kitty Hawk
G. Cherokee Indian Reservation
H. Alamance Battlefield
I. Grandfather Mountain
J. Chimney Rock
K. Nantahala Gorge

Words: gorge   swamp

Answer Key

U.S. Map Skills

Grades 5-8

Alabama

Capitol is Montgomery

4

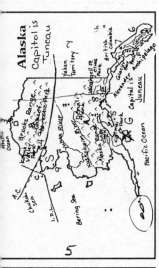

Alaska

Capitol is Juneau

5

Arizona

Capitol is Phoenix

6

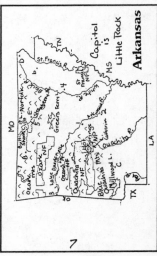

Arkansas

Capitol is Little Rock

7

California

Capitol is Sacramento

8

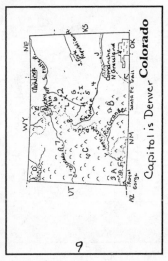

Colorado

Capitol is Denver

9

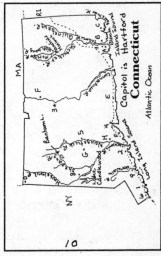

Connecticut

Capitol is Hartford

10

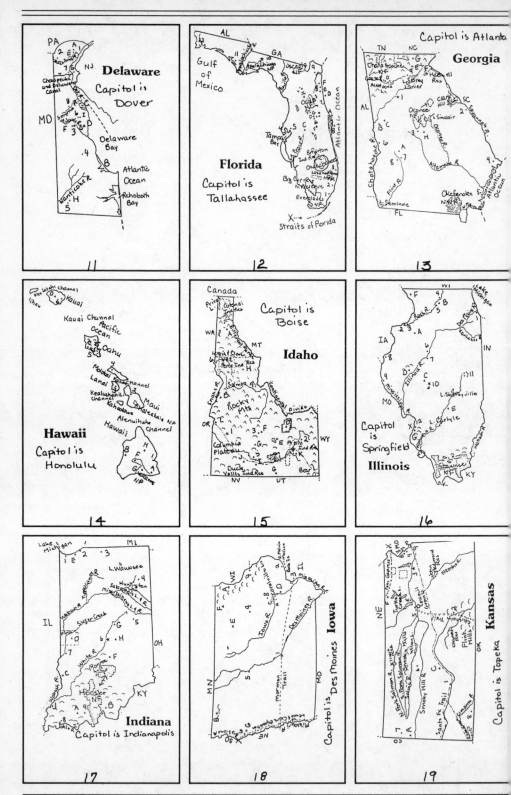

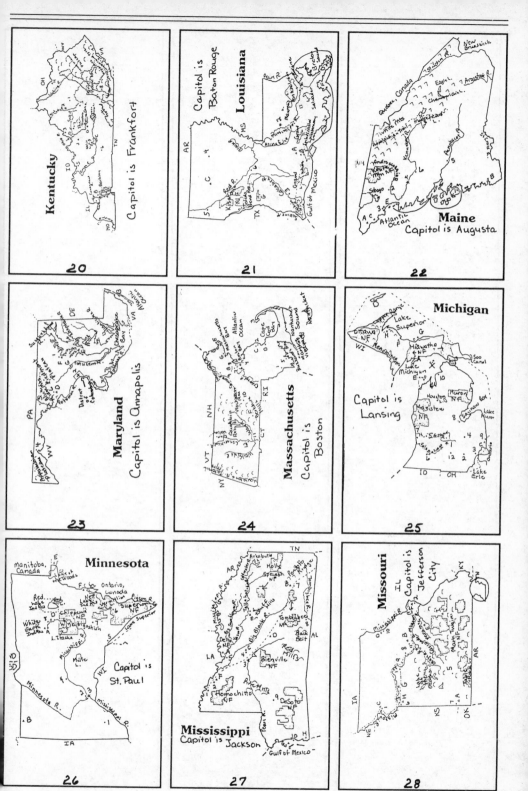

Kentucky Capitol is Frankfort

20

Capitol is Baton Rouge **Louisiana**

21

Maine Capitol is Augusta

22

Maryland Capitol is Annapolis

23

Massachusetts Capitol is Boston

24

Michigan Capitol is Lansing

25

Minnesota Capitol is St. Paul

26

Mississippi Capitol is Jackson

27

Missouri Capitol is Jefferson City

28

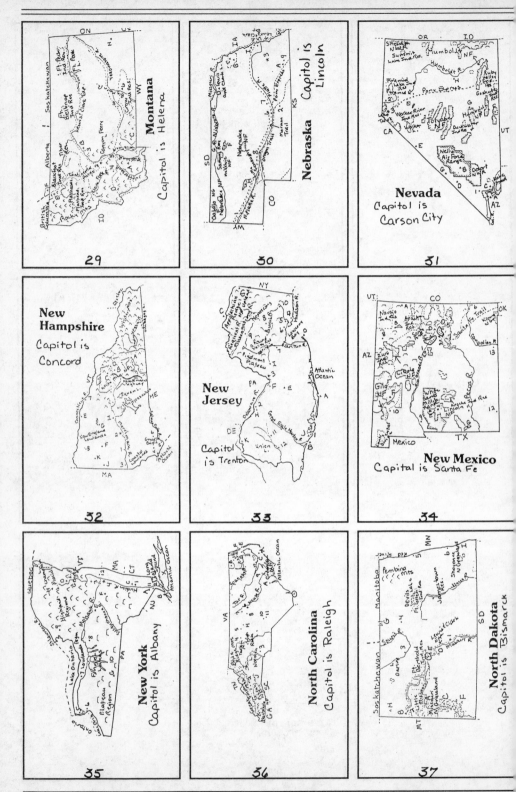

Montana
Capitol is Helena

29

Nebraska Capitol is
Lincoln

30

Nevada
Capitol is
Carson City

31

New Hampshire
Capitol is
Concord

32

New Jersey
Capitol
is Trenton

33

New Mexico
Capital is Santa Fe

34

New York
Capitol is Albany

35

North Carolina
Capitol is Raleigh

36

North Dakota
Capitol is Bismarck

37

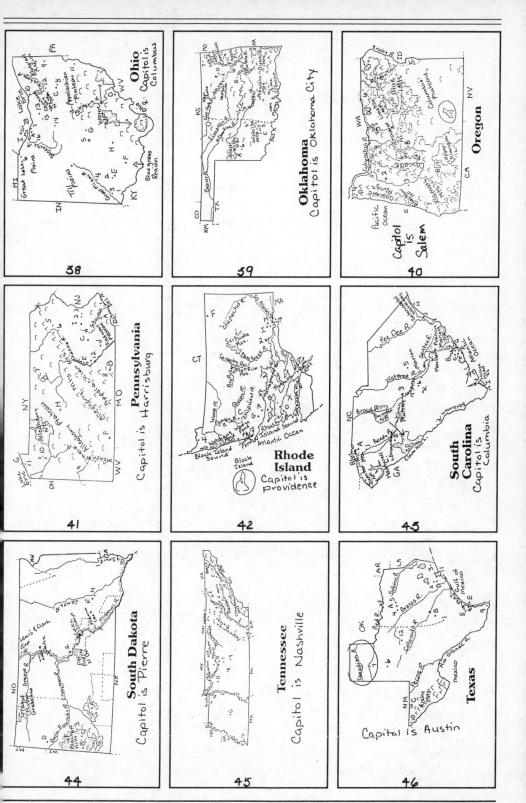

Ohio
Capitol is Columbus

38

Oklahoma
Capitol is Oklahoma City

39

Oregon
Capitol is Salem

40

Pennsylvania
Capitol is Harrisburg

41

Rhode Island
Capitol is Providence

42

South Carolina
Capitol is Columbia

43

South Dakota
Capitol is Pierre

44

Tennessee
Capitol is Nashville

45

Texas
Capital is Austin

46

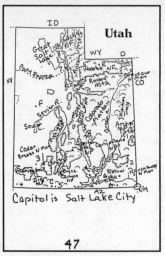

Utah

Capitol is Salt Lake City

47

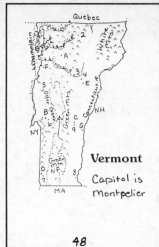

Vermont

Capitol is Montpelier

48

Virginia

Capitol is Richmond

49

Washington

Capitol is Olympia

50

West Virginia

Capitol is Charleston

51

Wisconsin

Capitol is Madison

52

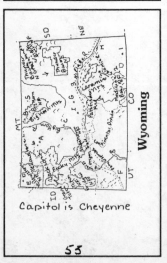

Wyoming

Capitol is Cheyenne

55

Geographical Terms

Draw lines connecting the geographical words with their proper definitions.

1. confluence — 3 — a land area having a level surface raised sharply above adjacent land
2. delta — 10 — a group of islands
3. plateau — 5 — a long narrow inlet from the sea between steep cliffs and slopes
4. portage — 6 — a cactus of the southwestern U.S. and Mexico that has a trunk up to 60 feet
5. fjord — 13 — a deep narrow valley with steep sides
6. saguaro — 11 — a high steep bank
7. bayou — 8 — a long wide ocean inlet
8. sound — 14 — a point of land projecting into a body of water
9. lowland — 12 — a vent in the earth's crust from which molten hot rock and steam issue
10. archipelago — 1 — a flowing together of two or more streams
11. bluff — 15 — a very hard quartz that sparks when struck with steel
12. volcano — 7 — a marshy body of water flowing to a lake or river
13. canyon — 2 — the water deposited at the mouth of a river
14. cape — 16 — a territorial region with a distinguishing character
15. flint — 9 — a low or level country
16. district — 17 — a piece of land jetting into the water
17. peninsula — 4 — the carrying of boats over land from one body of water to another

54

Geographical Terms

18. fossil — 30 — a large evergreen tree which includes the redwood
19. urban — 26 — an enclosed water area
20. bluegrass — 22 — an isolated hill or mountain with steep sides
21. quarry — 18 — a remnant of a plant or animal of past geologic ages that has been preserved in the earth's crust
22. butte — 27 — a natural spring that sets forth jets of heated water
23. chasm — 23 — a deep cleft in the earth
24. lignite — 19 — relating to a city
25. badlands — 28 — a deep gulley cut by an intermittent stream
26. basin — 24 — a low-grade brownish-black coal
27. geyser — 20 — a type of folk music played on banjos and guitars
28. arroyo — 29 — a mineral used in plaster of paris
29. gypsum — 25 — a region of scanty vegetation and fantastically formed hills
30. sequoia — 21 — an open excavation for obtaining building stone, slate, or limestone

55

State Capitals and Postal Abbreviations

Fill in the capital and postal abbreviation of each state.

	CAPITAL	POSTAL ABBREVIATION
Alabama	Montgomery	AL
Alaska	Juneau	AK
Arizona	Phoenix	AZ
Arkansas	Little Rock	AR
California	Sacramento	CA
Colorado	Denver	CO
Connecticut	Hartford	CT
Delaware	Dover	DE
Florida	Tallahassee	FL
Georgia	Atlanta	GA
Hawaii	Honolulu	HI
Idaho	Boise	ID
Illinois	Springfield	IL
Indiana	Indianapolis	IN
Iowa	Des Moines	IA
Kansas	Topeka	KS
Kentucky	Frankfort	KY
Louisiana	Baton Rouge	LA
Maine	Augusta	ME
Maryland	Annapolis	MD
Massachusetts	Boston	MA
Michigan	Lansing	MI
Minnesota	St. Paul	MN

56

	CAPITAL	POSTAL ABBREVIATION
Mississippi	Jackson	MS
Missouri	Jefferson City	MO
Montana	Helena	MT
Nebraska	Lincoln	NE
Nevada	Carson City	NV
New Hampshire	Concord	NH
New Jersey	Trenton	NJ
New Mexico	Santa Fe	NM
New York	Albany	NY
North Carolina	Raleigh	NC
North Dakota	Bismarck	ND
Ohio	Columbus	OH
Oklahoma	Oklahoma City	OK
Oregon	Salem	OR
Pennsylvania	Harrisburg	PA
Rhode Island	Providence	RI
South Carolina	Columbia	SC
South Dakota	Pierre	SD
Tennessee	Nashville	TN
Texas	Austin	TX
Utah	Salt Lake City	UT
Vermont	Montpelier	VT
Virginia	Richmond	VA
Washington	Olympia	WA
West Virginia	Charleston	WV
Wisconsin	Madison	WI
Wyoming	Cheyenne	WY

57

Product Map

Research to find out one product for each state. Create your own symbol for each product and draw it in the appropriate state(s). Some of your symbols could be used more than once.

Answers will vary

60

Product Map, continued

Using the map on page 60, fill in the symbol and state sections of the chart below. Leave the product section blank. Exchange with someone to see if you can guess what product is being represented.

Symbol	State	Product	Symbol	State	Product
	Answers				
	will				
	Vary				

61

State Symbols

Below and on pages 63 through 67, label each state and its bird and flower.

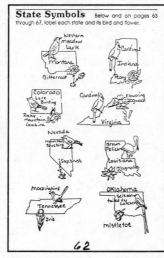

62

State Symbols, continued

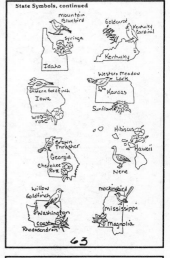

63

State Symbols, continued

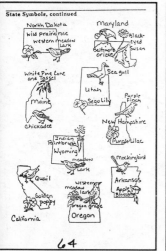

64

State Symbols, continued

65

State Symbols, continued

66

Page 67 — State Symbols, continued

State Symbols, continued

Connecticut — Robin
Hawthorn
Missouri — Bluebird
Illinois — Cardinal / Violet
mountain Laurel
Hermit Thrush — Vermont — Red Clover
Delaware — Blue Hen Chicken
Peach Blossom
Massachusettes — Mayflower
Chickadee
Michigan — Cardinal
apple blossom / robin
West Virginia
Rhododendron

67

Page 69

Color the Great Lakes blue and write their letters below on the map.

Trace over the rivers with blue and write their letters below in the correct circles on the map.

Color the mountain ranges purple and write their letters below in the correct squares on the map.

A. Lake Superior
B. Lake Huron
C. Lake Erie
D. Lake Michigan
E. Lake Ontario
F. Ohio River
G. Missouri River
H. Arkansas River
I. Red River
J. Colorado River
K. Rio Grande River
L. Mississippi River
M. Snake River
N. Platte River
O. Columbia River
P. Coastal Mountains
Q. Rocky Mountains
R. Sierra Nevadas
S. Appalachians
T. Cascade Mountains

Which states touch Canadian soil? Alaska, Washington, Idaho, Montana, North Dakota, Minnesota, Michigan, New York, Vermont, New Hampshire, Maine

Which states touch Mexican soil? California, Arizona, New Mexico, Texas

Which state is not part of the North American continent? Hawaii

What is the country's capital? Washington D.C.

Locate the following points of interest. Write their numbers below next to the symbols that represent them.

1. Sears Tower
2. Everglades National Park
3. Mammoth Cave
4. White Sands
5. United Nations
6. Kenai Fjords
7. Custer Battlefield
8. Fort Sumter

69

Page 70

List the bordering states, countries, and bodies of water of . . .

1. Alabama — north Tennessee — south Florida — east Georgia — west Mississippi — body of water Gulf of Mexico
2. Alaska — east Canada — body of water Arctic Ocean
3. Arizona — north Utah — east New Mexico — southwest California — northwest Nevada
4. Arkansas — north Missouri — south Louisiana — northeast Tennessee — southeast Mississippi — west Oklahoma
5. California — north Oregon — east Nevada — southeast Arizona — body of water Pacific Ocean
6. Colorado — north Wyoming — Nebraska — south New Mexico — Oklahoma — east Kansas — west Utah
7. Connecticut — north Massachusetts — east Rhode Island — body of water Atlantic Ocean
8. Delaware — north Pennsylvania — west & south Maryland — body of water Atlantic Ocean
9. Florida — north Alabama — Georgia — bodies of water Gulf of Mexico Atlantic Ocean
10. Georgia — north Tennessee — North Carolina — south Florida — northeast South Carolina — west Alabama — body of water Atlantic Ocean
11. Hawaii — body of water Pacific Ocean
12. Idaho — north Canada — Montana — southeast Wyoming — southwest Oregon — northwest Washington — west Nevada — Utah
13. Illinois — north Wisconsin — south Kentucky — northwest Iowa — southwest Missouri — east Indiana — body of water Lake MI.
14. Indiana — north Michigan — south Kentucky — east Ohio — west Illinois — body of water Lake Michigan
15. Iowa — north Minnesota — south Missouri — northeast Wisconsin — southeast Illinois — northwest South Dakota — southwest Nebraska

70

Page 71

16. Kansas — north Nebraska — south Oklahoma — east Missouri — west Colorado
17. Kentucky — north Illinois, Indiana, Ohio — south Tennessee — west Missouri — east West Virginia — Virginia
18. Louisiana — north Arkansas — east Mississippi — west Texas — body of water Gulf of Mexico
19. Maine — north Canada — southwest New Hampshire — body of water Atlantic Ocean
20. Maryland — north Pennsylvania — east Delaware — south Virginia — west West Virginia — body of water Atlantic Ocean
21. Massachusetts — north Vermont — New Hampshire — south Connecticut — Rhode Island — east New York — body of water Atlantic O.
22. Michigan — north Indiana — Ohio — west Wisconsin — bodies of water Lake Huron Lake Erie
23. Minnesota — north Canada — south Iowa — east Wisconsin — body of water Lake Superior — northwest N. Dakota — southwest S. Dakota
24. Mississippi — north Tennessee — east Alabama — northwest Arkansas — southwest Louisiana — body of water Gulf of Mexico
25. Missouri — north Iowa — south Arkansas — east Illinois — northwest Nebraska — southeast Kentucky — Tennessee — southwest Kansas
26. Montana — north Canada — south Wyoming — west Idaho — southeast S. Dakota — northeast N. Dakota
27. Nebraska — north S. Dakota — south Kansas — northeast Iowa — southeast Missouri — northwest Wyoming — southwest Colorado
28. Nevada — north Oregon — Idaho — south Utah — southeast Arizona — west California
29. New Hampshire — north Canada — south Massachusetts — east Maine — west Vermont — body of water Atlantic Ocean

71

Page 72

30. New Jersey — north New York — west Pennsylvania — body of water Atlantic Ocean
31. New Mexico — north Colorado — east Arizona — northeast Oklahoma — southeast Texas — south Canada
32. New York — north Canada — south Pennsylvania — New Jersey — east Vermont — Massachusetts — Connecticut — bodies of water Lake Erie — Lake Ontario — Atlantic O.
33. North Carolina — north Virginia — west Tennessee — south South Carolina — Georgia — body of water Atlantic Ocean
34. North Dakota — north Canada — south South Dakota — east Minnesota — west Montana
35. Ohio — north Michigan — south Kentucky — northeast Pennsylvania — southeast W. Virginia — west Indiana — body of water Lake Erie
36. Oklahoma — north Kansas — Colorado — south Texas — northeast Missouri — west New Mexico — southeast Arkansas
37. Oregon — north Washington — east Idaho — south California — Nevada — body of water Pacific Ocean
38. Pennsylvania — north New York — east New Jersey — west Ohio — body of water Lake Erie — south W. Virginia — Maryland — Delaware
39. Rhode Island — north Massachusetts — west Connecticut — body of water Atlantic Ocean
40. South Carolina — north North Carolina — west Georgia — body of water Atlantic Ocean
41. South Dakota — north North Dakota — south Nebraska — northeast Minnesota — southeast Iowa — west Wyoming — Montana
42. Tennessee — north Kentucky — Virginia — east North Carolina — northwest Montana — south Mississippi — Alabama — Georgia
43. Texas — north Arkansas — west New Mexico — northeast Arkansas — southeast Louisiana — body of water Gulf of Mexico

72

Page 73

44. Utah — north Idaho — Wyoming — south Arizona — east Colorado — west Nevada
45. Vermont — north Canada — south Massachusetts — east New Hampshire — west New York
46. Virginia — north West Virginia — Maryland — south North Carolina — Tennessee — west Kentucky — body of water Atlantic O.
47. Washington — north Canada — south Oregon — east Idaho — body of water Pacific O.
48. West Virginia — north Pennsylvania — east Maryland — northwest Ohio — southwest Kentucky
49. Wisconsin — north Michigan — south Illinois — northwest Minnesota — southwest Iowa — bodies of water Lake Superior Lake Michigan
50. Wyoming — north Montana — west Idaho — northeast South Dakota — southeast Nebraska — south Utah — Colorado

73

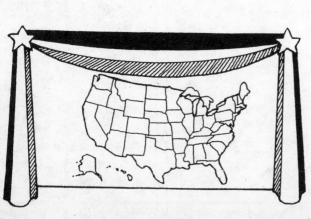

North Dakota

Postal Abbreviation: ND

Statehood: November 2, 1889 – 39th
Area: 70,665 square miles

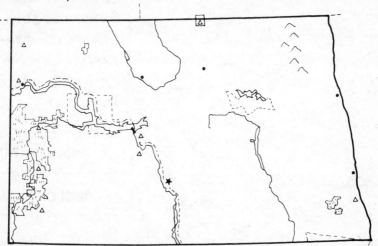

Write the names of the states, provinces of Canada and body of water that border North Dakota in their correct locations on the map.

Locate the following cities. Write their numbers below next to their dots on the map.

1. Bismarck   **3.** Minot   **5.** Grand Forks   The capital is
2. Williston   **4.** Rugby   **6.** Fargo

_____ .

Label the bodies of water, national grasslands and the mountains on the map.

Color the Indian reservations brown. Trace over the Lewis and Clark Expedition with brown. Circle Garrison Dam.

Points of Interest: Locate the following places. Write their letters below next to the symbols that represent them.

A. Theodore Roosevelt National Park

B. Fort Union Trading Post National Historic Site

C. Chateau De Mores Historic Site

D. Fort Mandan Historic Site

E. Knife River Indian Villages National Historic Site

Words: creeks   boulder   forks   lignite

Ohio

Postal Abbreviation: OH

Statehood: March 1, 1803 — 17th
Area: 41,222 square miles

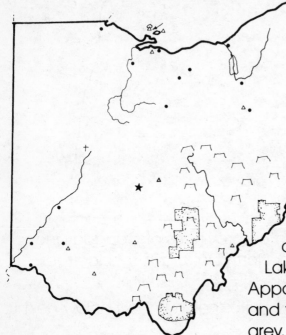

Write the names of the states and bodies of water that border Ohio in their correct locations on the map.

Label the bodies of water and the national forest and recreational area on the map.

Color the Till Plains orange, the Great Lakes Plains blue, the Appalachian Plateau green and the Bluegrass Region grey. Circle Kelley's Island.

Locate the following cities. Write their numbers below next to their dots on the map.

1. Cincinnati	6. Toledo	11. Steubenville	16. Fremont
2. Lebanon	7. Sandusky	12. Akron	
3. Hamilton	8. Canton	13. Elyria	The capital is
4. Dayton	9. Youngstown	14. Mansfield	
5. Columbus	10. Cleveland	15. Oberlin	_____

Points of Interest: Locate the following places. Write their letters below next to the symbols that represent them.

A. Blue Hole
B. Inscription Rock
C. Football Hall of Fame
D. Campus Martius Museum
E. Fort Ancient

F. Great Serpent Mound
G. Newark Earth Works
H. Mound City Group National Monument
I. Perry's Victory and International Peace Memorial

Words: valley   mound   bluegrass   till   grove

Oklahoma

Statehood: November 16, 1907 – 46th
Area: 69,919 square miles

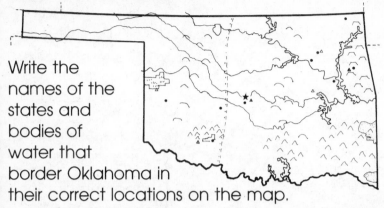

Write the names of the states and bodies of water that border Oklahoma in their correct locations on the map.

Locate the following cities. Write their numbers below next to their dots on the map.

1. Oklahoma City
2. Tulsa
3. Norman
4. Anadarko
5. Lawton
6. Elk City
7. Miami
8. Claremore
9. Talequah
10. Muskogee

The capital is _____.

Label the bodies of water, mountains and national forest and grassland on the map.

Trace over the Chisholm Trail with black. Color the Gypsum Hills brown, the Sandstone Hills red, the Prairie Plains green and the Ozark Plateau orange.

Points of Interest: Locate the following places. Write their letters below next to the symbols that represent them.

A. Washita Battlefield
B. Creek Capital
C. National Cowboy Hall of Fame
D. Will Rogers Memorial
E. Fort Sill Military Reservation and National Historic Landmark
F. Tsa-la-gi Indian Village

Words: gypsum   sandstone   prairie

Oregon

Postal Abbreviation: OR

Statehood: February 14, 1859 – 33rd
Area: 96,981 square miles

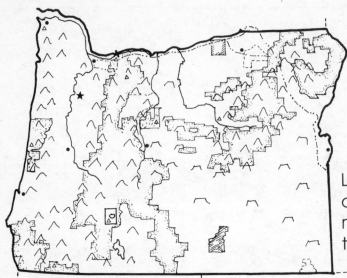

Write the names of the states and the bodies of water that border Oregon in their correct locations on the map.

Label the bodies of water and mountains on the map.

Locate the following cities. Write their numbers below next to the dots on the map.

1. Portland
2. Salem
3. Eugene
4. Astoria
5. Ontario
6. Pendleton
7. Coos Bay
8. Bend

The capital is
_____

Trace over the Oregon Trail with green. Color the Indian reservations brown. Circle Hart Mountain National Antelope Refuge. Mark an **X** on the U.S. Bombing Range. Color the national forests green.

Points of Interest: Locate the following places. Write their letters below next to the symbols that represent them on the map.

A. Mount Hood
B. Crater Lake National Park
C. Oregon Caves National Monument
D. Fort Clatsop National Memorial
E. Sea Lions Cave
F. John Day Fossil Park
G. Columbia River Gorge/ Bonneville Dam
H. Crooked River National Grassland

Words: crater   beds

Pennsylvania

Postal Abbreviation: PA

Statehood: December 12, 1787 – 2nd
Area: 45,333 square miles

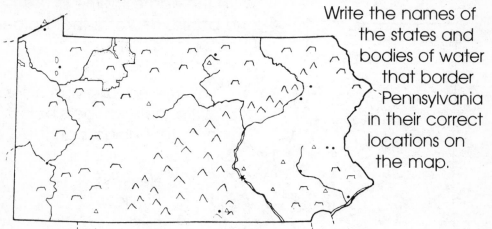

Write the names of the states and bodies of water that border Pennsylvania in their correct locations on the map.

Locate the following cities. Write their numbers below next to their dots on the map.

1. Philadelphia
2. Allentown
3. Bethlehem
4. Reading

5. Scranton
6. Wilkes-Barre
7. Wellsboro
8. Gettysburg

9. Pittsburgh
10. Titusville
11. Erie
12. Harrisburg

The capital is _____ .

Label the bodies of water, the national forest, two plateaus and two mountain ranges on the map.

Mark an **X** on the national recreation area. Color the Great Valley orange.

Points of Interest: Locate the following places. Write their letters below next to the symbols that represent them.

A. Valley Forge National Historic Park
B. Gettysburg National Military Park
C. Roadside America
D. Pine Creek Gorge
E. Rockville Bridge

F. Fort Necessity National Battlefield
G. Flagship Niagara
H. The Knobs
I. Hawk Mountain Sanctuary
J. Pennsylvania Farm Museum

Words: roadside   knob   burg

Rhode Island

Statehood: May 29, 1790 – 13th
Area: 1,210 square miles

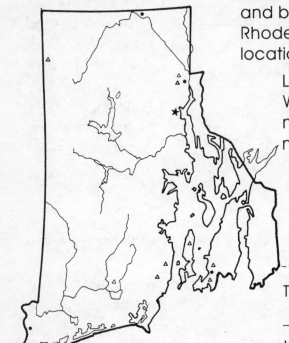

Write the names of the states and bodies of water that border Rhode Island in their correct locations on the map.

Locate the following cities. Write their numbers below next to their dots on the map.

1. Newport
2. Providence
3. Pawtucket
4. Westerly
5. Woonsocket
6. Warwick

The capital is

_____.

Label the bodies of water on the map.

★ State capital
• City
△ Points of Interest

Circle Block Island. Mark an **X** on Aquidneck Island. Color Conanicut Island red and Prudence Island orange. Color Narragansett Bay blue and Mount Hope Bay green. Write an **N** on Point Judith Neck.

Points of interest: Locate the following places. Write their letters below next to the symbols that represent them.

A. Gilbert Stuart Birthplace
B. Old Windmill
C. Great Swamp Fight Monument
D. Old Colony House

E. Old Stone Mill
F. Jerimoth Hill
G. University of Rhode Island
H. Eleazer Arnold House
I. Old Slater Mill

Words: pond neck

South Carolina

Postal Abbreviation: SC

Statehood: May 23, 1788 – 8th
Area: 31,055 square miles

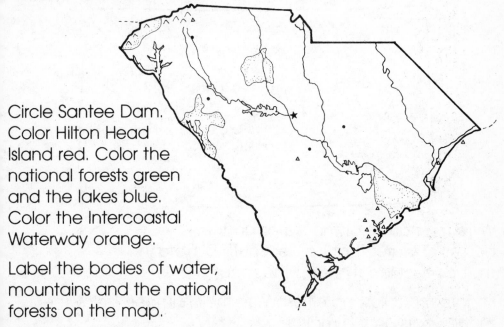

Circle Santee Dam.
Color Hilton Head
Island red. Color the
national forests green
and the lakes blue.
Color the Intercoastal
Waterway orange.

Label the bodies of water,
mountains and the national
forests on the map.

Write the names of the states and bodies of water that
border South Carolina in their correct locations on the map.

Locate the following cities. Write their numbers below next
to their dots on the map.

1. Greenville   4. Charleston   The capital is
2. Greenwood   5. Sumter
3. Columbia   6. Saint Matthews   _____.

Points of Interest: Locate the following places. Write their
letters below next to the symbols that represent them.

A. Chattooga Ridge
B. Middleton Place Gardens
C. Magnolia Gardens
D. Cypress Gardens
E. Fort Johnson
F. Fort Sumter
G. Fort Moultrie
H. Myrtle beach
I. Fort Pulaski National
   Monument
J. Brookgreen Gardens
K. Edisto Gardens

Words: intercoastal   waterway   reed   ridge

South Dakota

Postal Abbreviation: SD

Statehood: November 2, 1889 – 40th
Area: 77,047 square miles

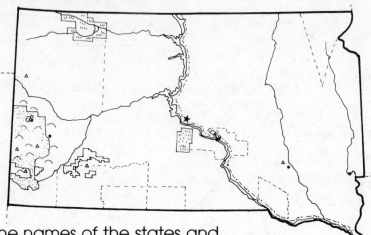

Write the names of the states and bodies of water that border South Dakota in their correct locations on the map.

Locate the following cities. Write their numbers below next to their dots on the map.

1. Sioux Falls   **3.** Rapid City   The capital is
2. Pierre   **4.** Mitchell   _____ .

Color the Indian reservations brown. Trace over the Lewis and Clark Expedition with brown. Circle Big Bend Dam. Mark an **X** on the Great Lakes of South Dakota.

Label the bodies of water, the national grasslands and the national forest on the map.

Points of Interest: Locate the following places. Write their letters below next to the symbols that represent them.

A. Badlands National Park
B. Jewel Cave National Monument
C. Mount Rushmore National Memorial
D. Geographic Center of the United States
E. Corn Palace
F. Deadwood
G. Fossil Cycad National Monument

Words: peak   cycad   badlands   traverse

Tennessee

Statehood: June 1, 1796 – 16th
Area: 42,114 square miles

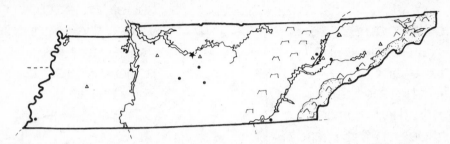

Write the names of the states and bodies of water that border Tennessee in their correct locations on the map.

Label the bodies of water, the mountain range and the national forest on the map.

Locate the following cities. Write their numbers below next to their dots on the map.

1. Nashville
2. Knoxville
3. Memphis
4. Gatlinburg
5. Oak Ridge
6. Chattanooga
7. Smyrna
8. Spring Hill
9. Murfreesboro

The capital is

_____ .

Color the Cumberland Plateau yellow and the Great Valley green. Mark an **X** on Great Smoky Mountains National Park. Color the Nashville Basin blue. Draw a red line on the western Highland Rim and an orange line on the eastern Highland Rim.

Points of Interest: Locate the following places. Write their letters below next to the symbols that represent them.

A. U.S. Atomic Energy Commission
B. The Hermitage
C. Andrew Johnson National Historic Site
D. Jewel Cave
E. Clingman's Dome
F. Lookout Mountain Caverns
G. Railroad Museum
H. Palace Caverns
I. Indian Cave

Words: ridge   cave   basin   cavern

Texas

Postal Abbreviation: TX

Statehood: December 29, 1845 – 28th
Area: 266,807 square miles

Write the names of the states, the country and the bodies of water that border Texas in their correct locations on the map.

Label the bodies of water, the mountain range and the national forest on the map.

Circle what is commonly called the ``Pan Handle.''
Trace over the Chisholm Trail with black. Color Big Bend National Park orange and Guadulupe Mountains National Park green.

Locate the following cities. Write their numbers below next to their dots on the map.

1. San Antonio
2. Houston
3. Beaumont
4. Fort Worth

5. Dallas
6. Lubbock
7. Amarillo
8. Corpus Christi

9. Brownsville
10. El Paso
11. Galveston
12. Abilene

The capital is _____ .

Points of Interest: Locate the following places. Write their letters below next to the symbols that represent them.

A. Six Flags over Texas
B. Aquarena Springs
C. Guadalupe Peak

D. N.A.S.A.
E. Padre Island National Seashore

Words: seashore   trail

Utah

Statehood: January 4, 1896 – 45th
Area: 84,899 square miles

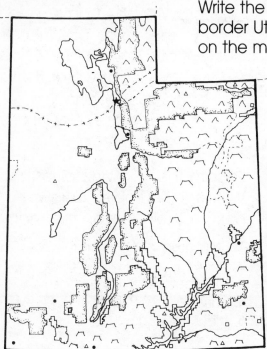

Write the names of the states that border Utah in their correct locations on the map.

Locate the following cities. Write their numbers below next to their dots on the map.

1. Moab   5. Kanab
2. Blanding   6. Provo
3. Cedar City   7. Salt Lake City
4. Saint George 8. Ogden

The capital is

_____ .

Label the bodies of water, mountain range, the plateau region, national parks and national monuments on the map.

Trace over the Pony Express with orange and the Mormon Trail with purple. Color the Cache National Forest blue, the Wasatch National Forest red, the Ashley National Forest grey, the Unita National Forest white, the Manti-la Sal National Forest orange, the Fishlake National Forest green and the Dixie National Forest purple. Color the Indian reservation brown. Circle what is commonly called the ``Four Corners'' area.

Points of Interest: Locate the following places. Write their letters below next to the symbols that represent them.

A. Glen Canyon National Recreation Area
B. Monument Valley
C. Indian Cliff Ruins

D. Flaming Gorge National Recreation Area
E. Kings Peak
F. Sevier Desert

Words: arch   reef   cedar   bridge

Vermont

Postal Abbreviation: VT

Statehood: March 4, 1791 – 14th
Area: 9,614 square miles

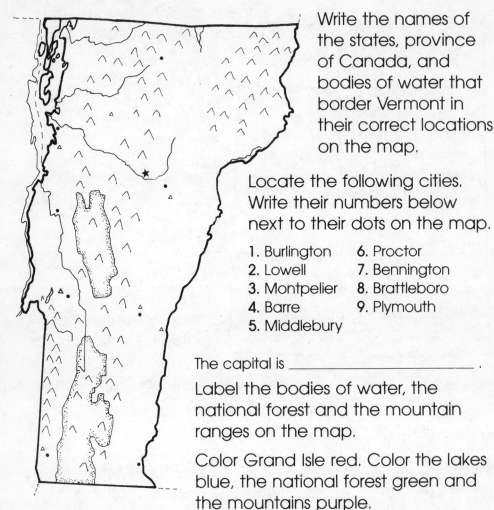

Write the names of the states, province of Canada, and bodies of water that border Vermont in their correct locations on the map.

Locate the following cities. Write their numbers below next to their dots on the map.

1. Burlington
2. Lowell
3. Montpelier
4. Barre
5. Middlebury
6. Proctor
7. Bennington
8. Brattleboro
9. Plymouth

The capital is _____.

Label the bodies of water, the national forest and the mountain ranges on the map.

Color Grand Isle red. Color the lakes blue, the national forest green and the mountains purple.

Points of Interest: Locate the following places. Write their letters below next to the symbols that represent them.

A. Smugglers Notch
B. Marble Quarries
C. Coolidge Birthplace
D. Bennington Battle Monument
E. Granite Quarries
F. Shelburne Museum
G. Old Constitution House

Words: notch   granite   quarry   isle

Virginia

Postal Abbreviation: VA

Statehood: June 25, 1788 – 10th
Area: 40,767 square miles

Write the names of the states, the mountain range, the capital and the bodies of water that border Virginia in their correct locations on the map.

Label the bodies of water and the national park on the map.

Locate the following cities. Write their numbers below next to their dots on the map.

1. Norfolk
2. Jamestown
3. Williamsburg
4. Richmond
5. Fredericksburg
6. Arlington
7. Charlottesville
8. Roanoke
9. Chincoteague
10. Appalachia
11. Cedar Bluff
12. Mount Solon

The capital is

_____ .

Color George Washington National Forest green and Jefferson National Forest red. Color Chesapeake Bay blue. Color the Coastal Plains yellow, the Piedmont Plateau brown and the Great Valley orange.

Points of Interest: Locate the following places. Write their letters below next to the symbols that represent them.

A. Natural Tunnel
B. Appomattox Court House National Historic Park
C. Monticello
D. George Washington Birthplace
E. Chesapeake Bay Bridge and Tunnel
F. Booker T. Washington Birthplace
G. Natural Chimneys
H. Tomb of the Unknown Soldier, Arlington Cemetery

Words: bluff   Appalachia

Washington

Postal Abbreviation: WA

Statehood: November 11, 1889 – 42nd
Area: 68,139 square miles

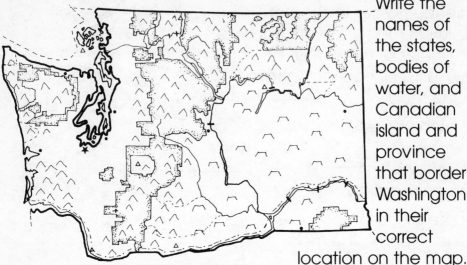

Write the names of the states, bodies of water, and Canadian island and province that border Washington in their correct location on the map.

Locate the following cities. Write their numbers below next to their dots on the map.

1. Tacoma
2. Walla-Walla
3. Seattle

4. Spokane
5. Olympia
6. Port Angeles

7. Wenatchee
8. Aberdeen
9. Ilwaco

The capital is _____ .

Trace the Lewis and Clark Expedition with brown. Color the national forests green and the national parks yellow. Color the Indian reservations brown. Circle the dams.

Label the bodies of water, the plateau and the mountain ranges on the map.

Points of Interest: Locate the following places. Write their letters below next to the symbols that represent them.

A Mount Ranier
B. San Juan Islands
C. Ross Lake National
     Recreation Area

D. Grand Coulee Dam
E. Maryhill Museum
F. Fort Vancouver National
     Historic Site

Words: dam   port   coulee

West Virginia

Postal Abbreviation: WV

Statehood: June 20, 1863 – 35th
Area: 24,123 square miles

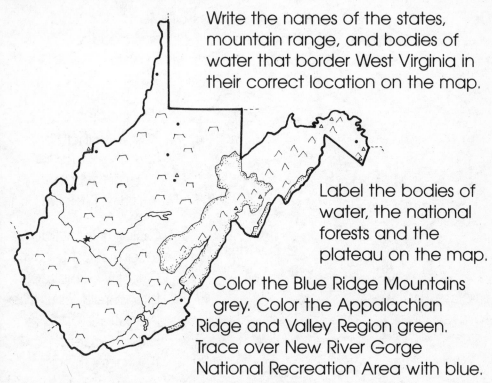

Write the names of the states, mountain range, and bodies of water that border West Virginia in their correct location on the map.

Label the bodies of water, the national forests and the plateau on the map.

Color the Blue Ridge Mountains grey. Color the Appalachian Ridge and Valley Region green. Trace over New River Gorge National Recreation Area with blue.

Locate the following cities. Write their numbers below next to their dots on the map.

1. Huntington
2. Parkersburg
3. Wheeling

4. Charleston
5. White Sulphur Springs
6. Martinsburg

7. Weston
8. Clarksburg
9. Morgantown

The capital is _____ .

Points of Interest: Locate the following places. Write their letters below next to the symbols that represent them.

A. Jacksons Mill
B. Seneca Rock
C. Cass Scenic Railroad
D. Blennerhassett Island
E. Harpers Ferry

F. Charles Town
G. Chesapeake and Ohio Canal National Historic Park
H. Berkely Springs

Words: sulphur   range   ferry

Wisconsin

Postal Abbreviation: WI

Statehood: May 29, 1848 – 30th
Area: 56,153 square miles

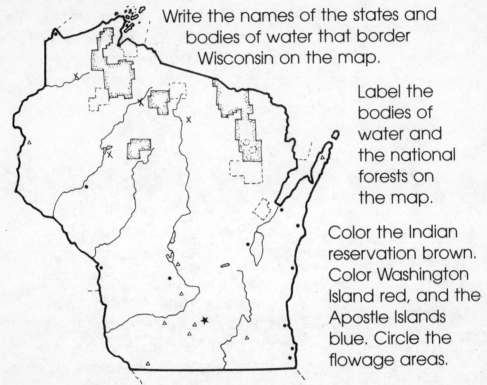

Write the names of the states and bodies of water that border Wisconsin on the map.

Label the bodies of water and the national forests on the map.

Color the Indian reservation brown. Color Washington Island red, and the Apostle Islands blue. Circle the flowage areas.

Locate the following cities. Write their numbers below next to their dots on the map.

1. Milwaukee
2. Manitowac
3. Superior
4. Eau Clair
5. Oshkosh
6. Kenosha
7. La Crosse
8. Racin
9. Madison
10. Sheboygan
11. Green Bay
12. Baraboo

The capital is

_____ .

Points of Interest: Locate the following places. Write their letters below next to the symbols that represent them.

A. Taliesin
B. Little Norway
C. Cave of the Mounds
D. Wisconsin Dells
E. Old World Wisconsin
F. Circus World Museum
G. Door Peninsula
H. Saint Croix Scenic National Waterway
I. Charles Mound

Words: dells   mound   flowage

Wyoming

Statehood: July 10, 1890 – 44th
Area: 97,809 square miles

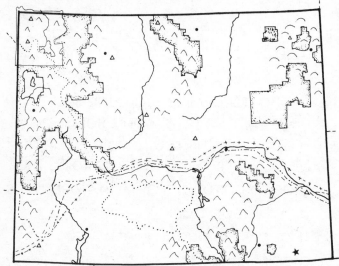

Write the names of the states that border Wyoming in their correct location.

Locate the following cities. Write their numbers below next to their dots on the map.

1. Cheyenne
2. Laramie
3. Casper
4. Sundance
5. Sheridan
6. Cody
7. Jackson
8. Green River

The capital is

_____

Label the bodies of water, national parks and grasslands, and mountain ranges on the map.

Color the Indian reservation brown. Trace over the Oregon Trail green, the Pony Express orange; the Mormon Trail red and the Continental Divide with blue. Color the national forests green.

Points of Interest: Locate the following places. Write their letters below next to the symbols that represent them.

A. Spirit Mountain Cavern
B. Medicine Wheel
C. Wind River Canyon
D. Hot Springs
E. Old Faithful Geyser
F. Fort Bridger
G. Hells Half Acre
H. Fort Laramie
I. Castle Gardens Petroglyph Site
J. Pinnacle Peaks

Words: intercoastal   waterway   reed   ridge

53

Geographical Terms

Write the number of each geographical word next to its proper definition.

1. confluence   _____ a land area having a level surface raised sharply above adjacent land

2. delta   _____ a group of islands

3. plateau   _____ a long narrow inlet from the sea between steep cliffs and slopes

4. portage   _____ a cactus of the southwestern U.S. and Mexico that has a trunk up to 60 feet

5. fjord   _____ a deep narrow valley with steep sides

   _____ a high steep bank

6. saguaro   _____ a long wide ocean inlet

7. bayou   _____ a point of land projecting into a body of water

8. sound   _____ a vent in the earth's crust from which molten hot rock and steam issue

9. lowland   _____ a flowing together of two or more streams

10. archipelago   _____ a very hard quartz that sparks when struck with steel

11. bluff   _____ a marshy body of water flowing to a lake or river

12. volcano   _____ the water deposited at the mouth of a river

13. canyon   _____ a territorial region with a distinguishing character

14. cape   _____ a low or level country

15. flint   _____ a piece of land jetting into the water

16. district   _____ the carrying of boats over land from one body of water to another

17. peninsula

Geographical Terms

18. fossil

19. urban

20. bluegrass

21. quarry

22. butte

23. chasm

24. lignite

25. badlands

26. basin

27. geyser

28. arroyo

29. gypsum

30. sequoia

____ a large evergreen tree which includes the redwood

____ an enclosed water area

____ an isolated hill or mountain with steep sides

____ a remnant of a plant or animal of past geologic ages that has been preserved in the earth's crust

____ a natural spring that sets forth jets of heated water

____ a deep cleft in the earth

____ relating to a city

____ a deep gulley cut by an intermittent stream

____ a low-grade brownish-black coal

____ a type of folk music played on banjos and guitars

____ a mineral used in plaster of Paris

____ a region of scanty vegetation and fantastically formed hills

____ an open excavation for obtaining building stone, slate, or limestone

State Capitals and Postal Abbreviations

Fill in the capital and postal abbrevation of each state.

	CAPITAL	POSTAL ABBREVIATION
Alabama		
Alaska		
Arizona		
Arkansas		
California		
Colorado		
Connecticut		
Delaware		
Florida		
Georgia		
Hawaii		
Idaho		
Illinois		
Indiana		
Iowa		
Kansas		
Kentucky		
Louisiana		
Maine		
Maryland		
Massachusetts		
Michigan		
Minnesota		

	CAPITAL	POSTAL ABBREVIATION
Mississippi		
Missouri		
Montana		
Nebraska		
Nevada		
New Hampshire		
New Jersey		
New Mexico		
New York		
North Carolina		
North Dakota		
Ohio		
Oklahoma		
Oregon		
Pennsylvania		
Rhode Island		
South Carolina		
South Dakota		
Tennessee		
Texas		
Utah		
Vermont		
Virginia		
Washington		
West Virginia		
Wisconsin		
Wyoming		

State Birds

Yellow Hammer
Willow Ptarmigan
Cactus Wren
Mockingbird (5)
California Valley Quail
Lark Bunting
Robin (3)
Blue Hen Chicken
Brown Thrasher
Nene (Hawaiian goose)
Mountain Bluebird (2)
Cardinal (6)

Eastern Goldfinch (2)
Western
   Meadowlark (5)
Kentucky Cardinal
Brown Pelican
Chickadee (2)
Baltimore Oriole
Common Loon
Bluebird (2)
Scissor-tailed
   Flycatcher
Purple Finch

Roadrunner
Ruffed Grouse
Rhode Island Red
Carolina Wren
Ring-necked
   Pheasant
Seagull
Hermit Thrush
Willow Goldfinch
Meadowlark

State Flowers

Camellia
Forget-Me-Not
Saguaro (Giant Cactus)
Apple Blossom (2)
Golden Poppy
Rocky Mountain
 Columbine
Mountain Laurel (2)
Peach Blossom
Orange Blossom
Cherokee Rose
Hibiscus
Syringa
Native Violet
Peony
Wild Rose
Sunflower
Goldenrod (2)
Magnolia (2)
White Pine Cone and Tassel
Black-eyed Susan
Mayflower
Pink and White Lady's Slipper
Hawthorn

Bitterroot
Sagebrush
Purple Lilac
Purple Violet
Yucca Flower
Rose
Flowering Dogwood
Wild Prairie Rose
Scarlet Carnation
Mistletoe
Oregon Grape
Violet
Carolina Jessamine
American Pasqueflower
Iris
Bluebonnet
Sego Lily
Red Clover
Dogwood
Coast Rhododendron
Rhododendron
Wood Violet
Indian Paintbrush

Numbers in parentheses indicate for how many states this is the state
bird or flower.

Fill in the name of each state and its capital. Do this from memory. Check your answers with the map on page 3.

Correct # of states _____   Correct # of capitals _____

Product Map

Research to find out one product for each state. Create your own symbol for each product and draw it in the appropriate state(s). Some of your symbols could be used more than once.

Product Map, continued

Using the map on page 60, fill in the symbol and state sections of the chart below. Leave the product section blank. Exchange with someone to see if you can guess what product is being represented.

Symbol	State	Product	Symbol	State	Product

State Symbols
Below and on pages 63 through 67, label each state and its bird and flower.

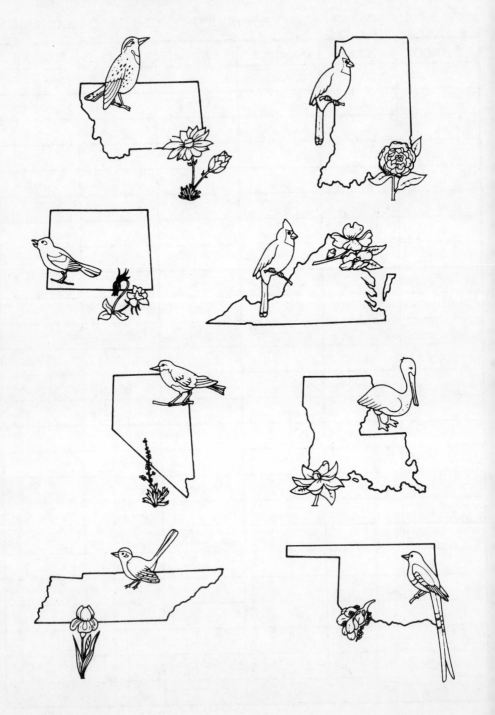

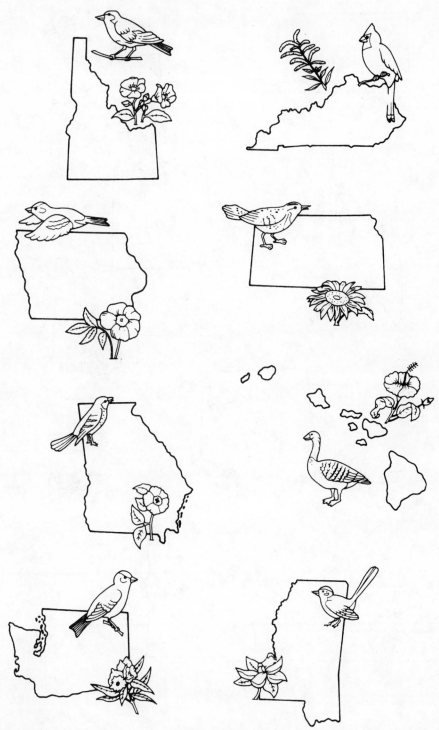

State Symbols, continued

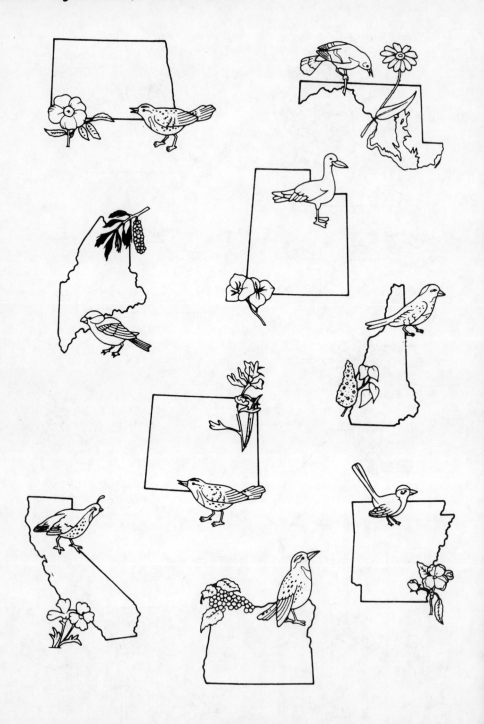

State Symbols, continued

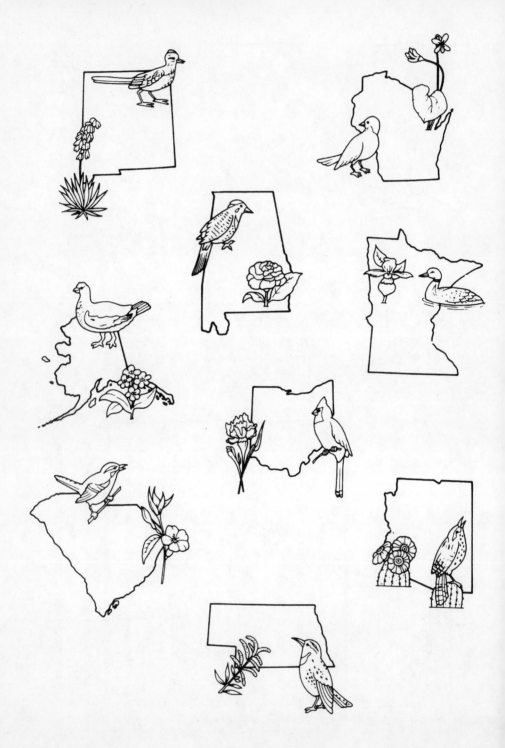

State Symbols, continued

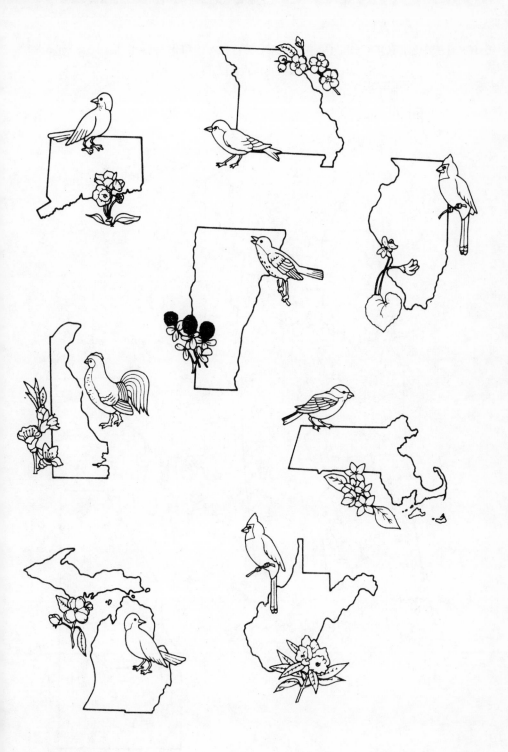

The United States of America

Area: 3,618,770 sq. mi.
Greatest Distances: North-South 1598 mi.
East-West 2807 mi.

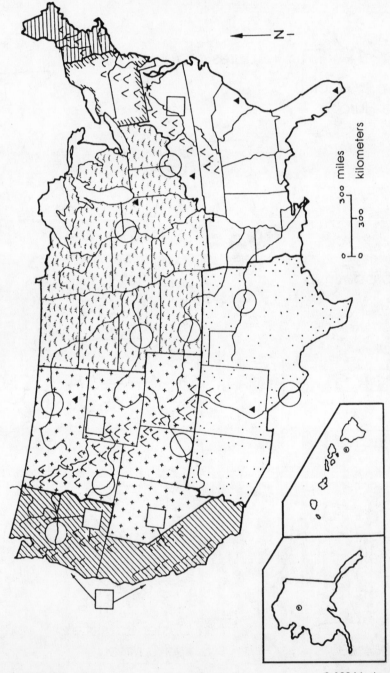

Color the Great Lakes blue and write their letters below on the map.

Trace over the rivers with blue and write their letters below in the correct circles on the map.

Color the mountain ranges purple and write their letters below in the correct squares on the map.

A. Lake Superior	K. Rio Grande River
B. Lake Huron	L. Mississippi River
C. Lake Erie	M. Snake River
D. Lake Michigan	N. Platte River
E. Lake Ontario	O. Columbia River
F. Ohio River	P. Coastal Mountains
G. Missouri River	Q. Rocky Mountains
H. Arkansas River	R. Sierra Nevadas
I. Red River	S. Appalachians
J. Colorado River	T. Cascade Mountains

Which states touch Canadian soil? _____

_____

Which states touch Mexican soil? _____

_____

Which state is not part of the North American continent?

_____

What is the country's capital? _____

Locate the following points of interest. Write their numbers below next to the symbols that represent them.

1. Sears Tower	5. United Nations
2. Everglades National Park	6. Kenai Fjords
3. Mammoth Cave	7. Custer Battlefield
4. White Sands	8. Fort Sumter

List the bordering states, countries, and bodies of water of . . .

1. Alabama   north_____   south_____
   east_____   west_____
   body of water_____

2. Alaska   east_____
   body of water_____

3. Arizona   north_____   east_____
   southwest_____   northwest_____

4. Arkansas   north_____   south_____
   northeast_____   southeast_____
   west_____

5. California   north_____   south_____
   northeast_____   southeast_____
   body of water_____

6. Colorado   north_____   _____
   south_____   _____
   east_____   west_____

7. Connecticut   north_____   east_____
   west_____   body of water_____

8. Delaware   north_____   west & south_____
   body of water_____

9. Florida   north_____   _____
   bodies of water   _____   _____

10. Georgia   north_____   _____
   south_____   northeast_____
   west_____   body of water_____

11. Hawaii   body of water_____

12. Idaho   north_____   northeast_____
   southeast_____   southwest_____
   northwest_____
   south_____   _____

13. Illinois   north_____   south_____
   northwest_____   southwest_____
   east_____   body of water_____

14. Indiana   north_____   south_____
   east_____   west_____
   body of water_____

15. Iowa   north_____   south_____
   northeast_____   southeast_____
   northwest_____   southwest_____

16. Kansas   north_____   south_____
                east_____   west_____
17. Kentucky   north _____ _____ _____
                south_____   west_____
                east_____   _____
18. Louisiana   north_____   east_____
                west_____   body of water_____
19. Maine   north_____   southwest_____
                body of water_____
20. Maryland   north_____   east_____
                south_____   west_____
                body of water_____
21. Massachusetts north_____   _____
                south_____   _____
                west_____   body of water_____
22. Michigan   south_____   _____
                west_____
                bodies of water _____ _____ _____
23. Minnesota   north_____   south_____
                east_____   body of water_____
                northwest_____ southwest_____
24. Mississippi north_____   east_____
                northwest_____ southwest_____
                body of water_____
25. Missouri   north_____   south_____
                northeast_____ northwest_____
                southeast_____ _____
                southwest_____
26. Montana   north_____   south_____
                west_____   southeast_____
                northeast_____
27. Nebraska   north_____   south_____
                northeast_____ southeast_____
                northwest_____ southwest_____
28. Nevada   north_____   _____
                northeast_____ southeast_____
                west_____
29. New   north_____   south_____
    Hampshire   east_____   west_____
                body of water_____

30. New Jersey north_____ west_____
                body of water_____
31. New Mexico north_____ west_____
                northeast_____ southeast_____
                south_____
32. New York   north_____
                south _____ _____
                east _____ _____ _____
                bodies of water _____ _____ _____
33. North   north_____ west_____
    Carolina   south_____ _____
                body of water_____
34. North   north_____ south_____
    Dakota   east_____ west_____
35. Ohio   north_____ south_____
                northeast_____ southeast_____
                west_____ body of water_____
36. Oklahoma   north_____ _____
                south_____ northeast_____
                west_____ southeast_____
37. Oregon   north_____ east_____
                south_____ _____
                body of water_____
38. Pennsylvania north_____ east_____
                west_____ body of water_____
                south _____ _____ _____
39. Rhode   north_____ west_____
    Island   body of water_____
40. South   north_____ west_____
    Carolina   body of water_____
41. South   north_____ south_____
    Dakota   northeast_____ southeast_____
                west_____ _____
42. Tennessee   north_____ _____
                east_____
                northwest_____ southwest_____
                south _____ _____ _____
43. Texas   north_____ west_____
                northeast_____ southeast_____
                body of water_____